Keto Chaffle Recipes Cookbook:

100+ Quick, Easy and Mouth-Watering Ketogenic Waffles to Lose Weight with Taste

|2021 Edition|

Table Of Contents

Legal & Disclaimer

The information contained in this book and its contents is not designed to replace or take the place of any form of medical or professional advice; and is not meant to replace the need for independent medical, financial, legal or other professional advice or services, as may be required. The content and information in this book have been provided for educational and entertainment purposes only.

The content and information contained in this book has been compiled from sources deemed reliable, and it is accurate to the best of the Author's knowledge, information and belief. However, the Author cannot guarantee its accuracy and validity and cannot be held liable for any errors and/or omissions. Further, changes are periodically made to this book as and when needed. Where appropriate and/or necessary, you must consult a professional (including but not limited to your doctor, attorney, financial advisor or such other professional advisor) before using any of the suggested remedies, techniques, or information in this book.

Upon using the contents and information contained in this book, you agree to hold harmless the Author from and against any damages, costs, and expenses, including any legal fees potentially resulting from the application of any of the information provided by this book. This disclaimer applies to any loss, damages or injury caused by the use and application, whether directly or indirectly, of any advice or information presented, whether for breach of contract, tort, negligence, personal injury, criminal intent, or under any other cause of action.

You agree to accept all risks of using the information presented inside this book.

You agree that by continuing to read this book, where appropriate and/or necessary, you shall consult a professional (including but not limited to your doctor, attorney, or financial advisor or such other advisor as needed) before using any of the suggested remedies, techniques, or information in this book.

Introduction

Keto chaffles have taken the world by storm. Made with just two main ingredients, egg and butter, they can be prepared easily at home. You can eat them as sweet desserts, as a breakfast food, or as a snack. Chaffles are perfectly healthy foods that follow the ketogenic diet recommendations.

They are high-fat, protein, and low-carbohydrate foods that can show the body how to use fat as an alternative source of fuel to produce energy and burn fat.

"Thank you for purchasing this book."

In this book, I will discuss chaffles and explain how they are different than waffles. I will explain the various types of chaffles you can make easily at home. I will also go deep into the ketogenic diet and discuss its many advantages.

Finally, I will also share many mouth-watering Keto Chaffle recipes that are all easy to prepare.

For each recipe, I will provide a list of ingredients and detailed step-by-step instructions.

I am sure you will find this book very useful.

"Happy reading!"

Chapter 1: First of all, What is a Chaffle?

These "Chaffles" are nothing more than waffles made with cheese. Hence the name "Chaffle" which derives from the union "Cheese" + "Waffle". People tied to the keto diet usually love chaffles.

Grated cheese is a main ingredient in chaffle.

It's made with an egg and cheese batter instead of the flour-based batter you'll find in waffles. The high flour content in waffles adds a lot of carbohydrates, making them unhealthy according to the recommendations of the keto diet. Chaffles, on the other hand, have no flour. You can tell they're low-carb waffles with cheese.

The chaffles are extremely delicious. You won't realize that what you are actually eating is cheese eggs or cheese waffles. There are hundreds of chaffle recipes available, so you'll never miss out on options when you want to make one. There are also chaffles without cheese, for those who want to avoid or limit their intake of grated cheese.

Chapter 2: Benefits of Keto Diet

The Keto diet has become so popular in recent years because of the success people have noticed. Not only have they lost weight, but scientific studies show that the Keto diet can help you improve your health in many others. As when starting any new diet or exercise routine, there may seem to be some disadvantages, so we will go over those for the Keto diet. But most people agree that the benefits outweigh the change period!

Benefits/ Advantages

Losing weight: for most people, this is the foremost benefit of switching to Keto! Their previous diet method may have stalled for them, or they were noticing weight creeping back on. With Keto, studies have shown that people have been able to follow this diet and relay fewer hunger pangs and suppressed appetite while losing weight at the same time!

You are minimizing your carbohydrate intake, which means more occasional blood sugar spikes. Often, those fluctuations in blood sugar levels make you feel hungrier and more prone to snacking in between meals. Instead, by guiding the body towards ketosis, you are eating a more fulfilling diet of fat and protein and harnessing energy from ketone molecules instead of glucose. Studies show that low-carb diets effectively reduce visceral fat (the fat you commonly see around the abdomen increases as you become obese). This reduces your risk of obesity and improves your health in the long run.

Reduce the Risk of Type 2 Diabetes: The problem with carbohydrates is how unstable they make blood sugar levels. This can be very dangerous for people who have diabetes or are pre-diabetic because of unbalanced blood sugar levels or family history. Keto is an excellent option because of the minimal intake of carbohydrates it requires. Instead, you are harnessing most of your calories from fat or protein, which will not cause blood sugar spikes and, ultimately, less pressured the pancreas to secrete insulin.

Many studies have found that diabetes patients who followed the Keto diet lost more weight and eventually reduced their fasting glucose levels. This is monumental news for patients with unstable blood sugar levels or hopes to avoid or reduce their diabetes medication intake.

Improve cardiovascular risk symptoms to lower your chances of having heart disease: Most people assume that following Keto is so high in fat content has to increase your risk of coronary heart disease or heart attack. But the research proves otherwise! Research shows that switching to Keto can lower your blood pressure, increase your HDL good cholesterol, and reduce your triglyceride fatty acid levels.

That's because the fat you are consuming on Keto is healthy and high-quality fats, so they reverse many unhealthy symptoms of heart disease. They boost your "good" HDL cholesterol numbers and decrease your "bad" LDL cholesterol numbers. It also reduces the level of triglyceride fatty acids in the bloodstream. A top-level of these can lead to stroke, heart attack, or premature death. And what are the top levels of fatty acids linked to?

High Consumption of Carbohydrates: With the Keto diet, you are drastically cutting your intake of carbohydrates to improve fatty acid levels and improve other risk factors. A 2018 study on the Keto diet found that it can improve 22 out of 26 risk factors for cardiovascular heart disease! These factors can be critical to some people, especially those who have a history of heart disease in their family.

Increases the Body's Energy Levels: Let's briefly compare the difference between the glucose molecules synthesized from a high carbohydrate intake versus ketones produced on the Keto diet. The liver makes ketones and use fat molecules you already stored. This makes them much more energy-rich and an endless source of fuel compared to glucose, a simple sugar molecule.

These ketones can give you a burst of energy physically and mentally, allowing you to have greater focus, clarity, and attention to detail.

Decreases inflammation in the body: Inflammation on its own is a natural response by the body's immune system, but when it becomes uncontrollable, it can lead to an array of health problems, some severe and some minor. The health concerns include acne, autoimmune conditions, arthritis, psoriasis, irritable bowel syndrome, and even acne and eczema.

Often, removing sugars and carbohydrates from your diet can help patients of these diseases avoid flare-ups - and the delightful news is Keto does just that! A 2008 research study found that Keto decreased a blood marker linked to high inflammation in the body by nearly 40%. This is glorious news for people who may suffer from inflammatory disease and want to change their diet to improve.

Increases your mental Functioning Level: As we elaborated earlier, the energy-rich ketones can boost the body's physical and mental levels of alertness. Research has shown that Keto is a much better energy source for the brain than simple sugar glucose molecules are. With nearly 75% of your diet coming from healthy fats, the brain's neural cells and mitochondria have a better source of energy to function at the highest level. Some studies have tested patients on the Keto diet and found they had higher cognitive functioning, better memory recall, and were less susceptible to memory loss. The Keto diet can even decrease the occurrence of migraines, which can be very detrimental to patients.

Decreases risk of diseases like Alzheimer's, Parkinson's, and epilepsy. They created the Keto diet in the 1920s to combat epilepsy in children. From there, research has found that Keto can improve your cognitive functioning level and protect brain cells from injury or damage. This is very good to reduce the risk of neurodegenerative disease, which begins in the brain because of neural cells mutating and functioning with damaged parts or lower than peak optimal functioning. Studies have found that the following Keto can improve the mental functioning of patients who suffer from diseases like Alzheimer's or Parkinson's.

These neurodegenerative diseases sadly have no cure, but the Keto diet could improve symptoms as they progress. Researchers believe that it's because of cutting out carbs from your diet, which reduces the occurrence of blood sugar spikes that the body's neural cells have to keep adjusting to.

Keto can regulate hormones in women who have PCOS (polycystic ovary syndrome) and PMS (pre-menstrual syndrome). Women who have PCOS suffer from infertility, which can be very heartbreaking for young couples trying to start a family. For this condition, there is no known cure, but we believe it's related to many similar diabetic symptoms like obesity and a high level of insulin. This causes the body to produce more sex hormones, which can lead to infertility.

The Keto diet paved its way as a popular way to regulate insulin and hormone levels and increase a woman's chances of getting pregnant.

Disadvantages

Your body will have a Changed period: It depends from person to person on the number of days that will be, but when you start any new diet or exercise routine, your body has to adjust to the new normal. With the Keto diet, you are drastically cutting your carbohydrates intake, so the body must adjust to that.

You may feel slow, weak, exhausted, and like you are not thinking as quick or fast as you used to. It just means that your body is making adjustments to Keto, and once this change period is done, you will see the weight loss results you expected.

If you are an athlete, you may need more carbohydrates: If you still want to try Keto as an athlete, you must talk to your nutritionist or trainer to see how the diet can be tweaked for you. Most athletes require a greater intake of carbs than the Keto diet requires, which means they may have to up their intake to ensure they have the energy for their training sessions.

High endurance sports (like rugby or soccer) and heavy weightlifting require more significant information on carbohydrates. If you're an athlete wanting to follow

Keto and gain the health benefits, it's crucial you first talk to your trainer before changing your diet.

You have to count your daily macros carefully: For beginners, this can be tough, and even people already on Keto can become lazy about this. People are often used to eating what they want without worrying about just how many grams of protein or carbs it contains. With Keto, be meticulous about counting your intake to ensure you are maintaining the Keto breakdown (75% fat, 20% protein, ~5% carbs). The closer you stick to this, the better results you will see regarding weight loss and other health benefits.

If your weight loss has stalled or you're not feeling as energetic as you hoped, it could be because your macros are off. Find a free calorie counting app that you look at the ingredients of everything you're eating and cooking.

Chapter 3 – How to make the Perfect Chaffle

Here are some tips that will help you make fantastic chaffles –

- Add a slice of chopped ham while mixing the egg and cheese. This will give you more protein and flavor. Those on a strict keto diet can also use bacon.

- Before adding the egg and cheese mixture, sprinkle some extra cheese on your waffle or chaffle maker. You will then have a savory and crispy chaffle.

- Don't open the waffle iron too early for checking. It should continue cooking until the chaffle is done and crisp. Let it cook for slightly longer for best results.

- Use mozzarella if you want your chaffle to be sweet. Cheddar cheese is good for savory chaffles. You can use Haloumi or goat cheese, but mozzarella is always the best option because it is mild and not as greasy as many other cheese varieties. Mozzarella will also reduce the eggy taste.

- Pepper jack cheese will give a slightly spicy taste.

Simple Chaffle Recipes

Layered Cheese Chaffles

Servings: 1
Cooking Time: 5 Minutes

Ingredients:

- 1 organic egg, beaten
- 1/3 cup Cheddar cheese, shredded
- ½ teaspoon ground flaxseed
- ¼ teaspoon organic baking powder
- 2 tablespoons Parmesan cheese, shredded

Directions:

Preheat a mini waffle iron and then grease it.

In a bowl, place all the ingredients except Parmesan and beat until well combined.

Place half the Parmesan cheese in the bottom of preheated waffle iron.

Place half of the egg mixture over cheese and top with the remaining Parmesan cheese.

Cook for about 3-minutes or until golden brown.

Serve warm.

Nutrition Info: Per Servings:
Calories: 264Net Carb: 1.Fat: 20g Saturated Fat: 11.1gCarbohydrates: 2.1gDietary Fiber: 0.4g Sugar: 0.6gProtein: 18.9g

Chaffle bagels

Servings: 2
Preparation time: 5 minutes
Nutritional Values: 322 kcal Calories | 23 g Fat | 5 g Carbs | 19 g Proteins

Ingredients

- 1 large egg
- 1 tsp of coconut flour
- 1 tsp of everything bagel seasoning (and as well as more, for serving)
- 1/2 cup of mozzarella cheese, finely shredded
- 2 tbsp of cream cheese

Directions

Turn on to preheat your waffle iron

Stir the coconut flour, egg as well as bagel seasoning together till fully mixed. Mix the cheese in

Pour half the mixture of the eggs in the waffle iron then cook for about 3 min

Put the waffle out and continue with the egg mixture leftover

Layer each waffle of cream cheese then, if needed, sprinkle with extra bagel seasoning

Notes

- To cut off a whole, from the waffle middle, use a sharp knife and make it look very much like a bagel, or just enjoy it like it is

Chaffles With Keto Ice Cream

Servings: 2
Cooking Time: 14 Minutes

Ingredients:

- 1 egg, beaten
- ½ cup finely grated mozzarella cheese
- ¼ cup almond flour
- 2 tbsp swerve confectioner's sugar
- 1/8 tsp xanthan gum

  Low-carb ice cream (flavor of your choice) for serving

Directions:

1. Preheat the waffle iron.
   In a medium bowl, mix all the ingredients except the ice cream.

   Open the iron and add half of the mixture. Close and cook until crispy, 7 minutes.

   Transfer the chaffle to a plate and make second one with the remaining batter.

   On each chaffle, add a scoop of low carb ice cream, fold into half-moons and enjoy.

Nutrition Info:
Calories 89Fats 48gCarbs 1.67gNet Carbs 1.37gProtein 5.91g

Cajun, shrimp and avocado chaffle sandwich

Servings: 2
Preparation time: 15 minutes
Nutritional Values: 488 kcal Calories | 32.22 g Fat | 6.01g Carbs | 47.59g Proteins

Ingredients
Cajun aromatized chaffle

- 4 eggs, should be large
- 2 cups shredded mozzarella part-skim cheese
- 1 tsp Seasoning of Cajun

Filling for sandwich

- 1-pound fresh shrimp peeled and deveined
- 1 tbsp of bacon (or avocado) grease
- 4 slices of bacon cooked
- 1 large sliced avocado
- 1/4 cup red onion, thinly sliced
- 1 dish bacon scallion cream cheese spread optional
- 1 Tsp Seasoning (Cajun)

Directions

Whisk the eggs together. Add 2 cups of mozzarella cheese with low moisture, and 1 tsp of Cajun seasoning. Put 1/4 cup of cheese and mixture of eggs over a mini waffle pan. Cook until the chaffle is browned. Repeat the process with the left egg and cheese batter

Add shrimp and combine it in a large bowl, with the remaining 1 tsp of Cajun seasoning. Garnish with salt and pepper. Fried in a pan over medium-high heat with bacon grease until the shrimp is translucent. Lift the fried shrimp and put aside. Let cool if desired

Place bacon scallion cream cheese over a side of a chaffle to create the Chaffle Sandwich: cover the top of the chaffle with shrimp, bacon, avocado and red onion. Cover with one more chaffle. Serve as you wish

Vanilla Mozzarella Chaffles

Servings: 2

Cooking Time: 12 Minutes

Ingredients:

- 1 organic egg, beaten
- 1 teaspoon organic vanilla extract
- 1 tablespoon almond flour
- 1 teaspoon organic baking powder
- Pinch of ground cinnamon
- 1 cup Mozzarella cheese, shredded

Directions:

Preheat a mini waffle iron and then grease it.

In a bowl, place the egg and vanilla extract and beat until well combined.

Add the flour, baking powder and cinnamon and mix well.

Add the Mozzarella cheese and stir to combine.

In a small bowl, place the egg and Mozzarella cheese and stir to combine.

Place half of the mixture into preheated waffle iron and cook for about 5-minutes or until golden brown.

Repeat with the remaining mixture.

Serve warm.

Nutrition Info: Per Servings:
Calories: 103Net Carb: 2.4gFat: 6.6g Saturated Fat: 2.3gCarbohydrates: 2.Dietary Fiber: 0.5g Sugar: 0.6gProtein: 6.8g

Bruschetta Chaffle

Servings: 2

Cooking Time: 5 Minutes

Ingredients:
- 2 basic chaffles
- 2 tablespoons sugar-free marinara sauce
- 2 tablespoons mozzarella, shredded
- 1 tablespoon olives, sliced
- 1 tomato sliced
- 1 tablespoon keto friendly pesto sauce
- Basil leaves

Directions:

Spread marinara sauce on each chaffle.

Spoon pesto and spread on top of the marinara sauce.

Top with the tomato, olives and mozzarella.

Bake in the oven for 3 minutes or until the cheese has melted.

Garnish with basil.

Serve and enjoy.

Nutrition Info:
Calories 182Total Fat 11g Saturated Fat 6.1g Cholesterol 30mg Sodium 508mg Potassium 1mgTotal Carbohydrate 3.1g Dietary Fiber 1.1g Protein 16.8g Total Sugars 1g

Egg-free Psyllium Husk Chaffles

Servings: 1

Cooking Time: 4 Minutes

Ingredients:

- 1 ounce Mozzarella cheese, shredded
- 1 tablespoon cream cheese, softened
- 1 tablespoon psyllium husk powder

Directions:

Preheat a waffle iron and then grease it.

In a blender, place all ingredients and pulse until a slightly crumbly mixture forms.

Place the mixture into preheated waffle iron and cook for about 4 minutes or until golden brown.

Serve warm.

Nutrition Info: Per Servings:
Calories: 137Net Carb: 1.3gFat: 8.8g Saturated Fat: 2gCarbohydrates: 1.3gDietary Fiber: 0g Sugar: 0gProtein: 9.5g

Mozzarella & Almond Flour Chaffles

Servings: 2
Cooking Time: 8 Minutes

Ingredients:

- ½ cup Mozzarella cheese, shredded
- 1 large organic egg
- 2 tablespoons blanched almond flour
- ¼ teaspoon organic baking powder

Directions:

Preheat a mini waffle iron and then grease it.

In a medium bowl, place all ingredients and with a fork, mix until well combined.

Place half of the mixture into preheated waffle iron and cook for about 4 minutes or until golden brown.

Repeat with the remaining mixture.

Serve warm.

Nutrition Info: Per Servings:
Calories: 98 Net Carb: 1.4g Fat: 7.1g Saturated Fat: 1g Carbohydrates: 2.2g
Dietary Fiber: 0.8g Sugar: 0.2g Protein: 7g

Keto chocolate chaffle recipe

Servings: 1
Preparation Time: 10 min
Nutritional Value: 672 kcal Calories | 70 g Fat | 11 g Carbs | 13 g Proteins

Ingredients

- 1/2 cup of sugar-free Choco-chips
- 1/2 cup of butter
- 3 eggs
- 1/4 cup of Truvia, or any other sweetener
- 1 tsp of vanilla extract

Directions

Melt the chocolate and butter in a secure bowl in the microwave for around 1 min

Remove it and mix it excellently
You ought to just use the heat inside chocolate and butter to melt the remaining clumps. You've over-cooked the chocolate when you microwave till it's melted it all

Then have a spoon, as well as start to mix

If necessary, add 10 sec but mix just before you intend to do so

Put the sweetener, vanilla and the eggs in a bowl and combine until it becomes light and foamy

In a gradual flow, add the melted chocolate and butter into the bowl, then beat it again till well absorbed

Place approximately 1/4 of the blend into a Mini Waffle Maker, then cook for 7-8 mins or till it becomes crispy

Should produce four waffles, leftover with just a little batter

Tips

- For higher results, serve this one with syrup or whipped cream when warm.
- Don't over-heat the chocolate; it will burn. Only cook and mix until soft & melted.

Pulled Pork Chaffle Sandwiches

Servings: 4
Cooking Time: 28 Minutes

Ingredients:

- 2 eggs, beaten
- 1 cup finely grated cheddar cheese
- ¼ tsp baking powder
- 2 cups cooked and shredded pork
- 1 tbsp sugar-free BBQ sauce
- 2 cups shredded coleslaw mix
- 2 tbsp apple cider vinegar
- ½ tsp salt
- ¼ cup ranch dressing

Directions:

Preheat the waffle iron.

In a medium bowl, mix the eggs, cheddar cheese, and baking powder.

Open the iron and add a quarter of the mixture. Close and cook until crispy, 7 minutes.

Transfer the chaffle to a plate and make 3 more chaffles in the same manner.

Meanwhile, in another medium bowl, mix the pulled pork with the BBQ sauce until well combined. Set aside.

Also, mix the coleslaw mix, apple cider vinegar, salt, and ranch dressing in another medium bowl.

When the chaffles are ready, on two pieces, divide the pork and then top with the ranch coleslaw. Cover with the remaining chaffles and insert mini skewers to secure the sandwiches.

Enjoy afterward.

Nutrition Info:
Calories 374Fats 23.61gCarbs 8.2gNet Carbs 8.2gProtein 28.05g

Cheddar & Egg White Chaffles

Servings: 4
Cooking Time: 12 Minutes

Ingredients:

- 2 egg whites
- 1 cup Cheddar cheese, shredded

Directions:

Preheat a mini waffle iron and then grease it.

In a small bowl, place the egg whites and cheese and stir to combine.

Place ¼ of the mixture into preheated waffle iron and cook for about 4 minutes or until golden brown.

Repeat with the remaining mixture.

Serve warm.

Nutrition Info: Per Servings:
Calories: 122Net Carb: 0.5gFat: 9.4g Saturated Fat:
Carbohydrates: 0.5gDietary Fiber: 0g Sugar: 0.3gProtein: 8.8g

Spicy Shrimp And Chaffles

Servings: 4
Cooking Time: 31 Minutes

Ingredients:

- For the shrimp:
- 1 tbsp olive oil
- 1 lb jumbo shrimp, peeled and deveined
- 1 tbsp Creole seasoning
- Salt to taste
- 2 tbsp hot sauce
- 3 tbsp butter
- 2 tbsp chopped fresh scallions to garnish
- For the chaffles:
- 2 eggs, beaten
- 1 cup finely grated Monterey Jack cheese

Directions:

For the shrimp:

Heat the olive oil in a medium skillet over medium heat.

Season the shrimp with the Creole seasoning and salt. Cook in the oil until pink and opaque on both sides, 2 minutes.

Pour in the hot sauce and butter. Mix well until the shrimp is adequately coated in the sauce, 1 minute.

Turn the heat off and set aside.

For the chaffles:

Preheat the waffle iron.

In a medium bowl, mix the eggs and Monterey Jack cheese.

Open the iron and add a quarter of the mixture. Close and cook until crispy, 7 minutes.

Transfer the chaffle to a plate and make 3 more chaffles in the same manner.

Cut the chaffles into quarters and place on a plate.

Top with the shrimp and garnish with the scallions.

Serve warm.

Nutrition Info:
Calories 342Fats 19.75gCarbs 2.8gNet Carbs 2.3gProtein 36.01g

Creamy Chicken Chaffle Sandwich

Servings: 2
Cooking Time: 10 Minutes

Ingredients:

- Cooking spray
- 1 cup chicken breast fillet, cubed
- Salt and pepper to taste
- ¼ cup all-purpose cream
- 4 garlic chaffles
- Parsley, chopped

Directions:

Spray your pan with oil.

Put it over medium heat.

Add the chicken fillet cubes.

Season with salt and pepper.

Reduce heat and add the cream.

Spread chicken mixture on top of the chaffle.

Garnish with parsley and top with another chaffle.

Nutrition Info:

Calories 273Total Fat 34g Saturated Fat 4.1g Cholesterol 62mg Sodium 373mg Total Carbohydrate 22.5g Dietary Fiber 1.1g Total Sugars 3.2g Protein 17.5g Potassium 177mg

Chaffle Cannoli

Servings: 4

Cooking Time: 28 Minutes

Ingredients:

- For the chaffles:
- 1 large egg
- 1 egg yolk
- 3 tbsp butter, melted
- 1 tbso swerve confectioner's
- 1 cup finely grated Parmesan cheese
- 2 tbsp finely grated mozzarella cheese
- For the cannoli filling:
- ½ cup ricotta cheese
- 2 tbsp swerve confectioner's sugar
- 1 tsp vanilla extract
- 2 tbsp unsweetened chocolate chips for garnishing

Directions:

1. Preheat the waffle iron.
2. Meanwhile, in a medium bowl, mix all the ingredients for the chaffles.
3. Open the iron, pour in a quarter of the mixture, cover, and cook until crispy, 7 minutes.
4. Remove the chaffle onto a plate and make 3 more with the remaining batter.
5. Meanwhile, for the cannoli filling:
6. Beat the ricotta cheese and swerve confectioner's sugar until smooth. Mix in the vanilla.
7. On each chaffle, spread some of the filling and wrap over.
8. Garnish the creamy ends with some chocolate chips.
9. Serve immediately.

Nutrition Info:

Calories 308Fats 25.05gCarbs 5.17gNet Carbs 5.17gProtein 15.18g

Banananut Chaffle

Servings: 2
Preparation time: 5 minutes
Nutritional Values: 119 kcal Calories | 8 g Fats | 2.7 g Carbs | 9 g Proteins

Ingredients

- 1 egg

- 1 tbsp of cream cheese, soft plus at room temperature 1 tbsp of cheesecake pudding, sugar-free, optional 1/2 cup of mozzarella cheese

- 1 tbsp of Monk Fruit
- 1/4 tsp of vanilla extract
- 1/4 tsp of banana extract

Toppings (optional)

- Caramel sauce, sugar-free
- Pecans

Directions

1. Heat up your waffle maker
2. Whisk the egg in a little bowl
3. Transfer the rest of the ingredient to the mixture of the eggs, then combine until completely incorporated
4. Transfer half the mixture to the maker then cook till it is golden brown, for a duration of four minutes. Remove the cooked chaffle as well as put the other portion of the mixture to make the next chaffle
5. 5. Top with the ingredients of your choice and serve hot

Strawberry Shortcake Chaffle Bowls

Servings: 4
Cooking Time: 28 Minutes

Ingredients:

- 1 egg, beaten
- ½ cup finely grated mozzarella cheese
- 1 tbsp almond flour
- ¼ tsp baking powder
- 2 drops cake batter extract
- 1 cup cream cheese, softened
- 1 cup fresh strawberries, sliced
- 1 tbsp sugar-free maple syrup

Directions:

1. Preheat a waffle bowl maker and grease lightly with cooking spray.
2. Meanwhile, in a medium bowl, whisk all the ingredients except the cream cheese and strawberries.
3. Open the iron, pour in half of the mixture, cover, and cook until crispy, 6 to 7 minutes.
4. Remove the chaffle bowl onto a plate and set aside.
5. Make a second chaffle bowl with the remaining batter.
6. To serve, divide the cream cheese into the chaffle bowls and top with the strawberries.
7. Drizzle the filling with the maple syrup and serve.

Nutrition Info:
Calories 235Fats 20.62gCarbs 5.9gNet Carbs 5gProtein 7.51g

Keto Chaffle Sausage And Egg Breakfast Sandwich

Servings: 2-3
Preparation time: 15 minutes
Nutritional values: 433 kcal Calories | 28.4g Fat | 8.5g Carbs | 17.6g Proteins

Ingredients

- 2 large raw eggs
- 2 tbsp of coconut flour
- 2 tbsp mayo
- 1/2 tsp baking powder
- 1 tsp absolute substitute icing sugar by swerve
- 1 x 2 patties brown banquet, and serve patties
- 3 /4 ounces - 2 slice American cheese slices

Directions

1. At medium-high temperature, preheat the waffle iron. In a big mixing dish, add two whites, coconut flour, mayo, baking powder and whisk

2. Whisk well. Let the batter stay for around 1 minute to thicken

3. Spray waffle iron with nonstick spray high heat grill. Put into hot waffle iron and cook as directed by iron. Take away waffles from the iron. Slice the chaffle in half

4. Meanwhile, use a nonstick cooking spray with a 4 oz ramekin. Add one egg and gently scramble it with a fork. Place completely cooked sausage patty in the middle and microwave for around 1 minute on 60 percent power before the egg is cooked through

5. Put egg and sausage with a slice of American cheese on a quarter of the chaffle. Repeat on the other sandwich with the cooking of another egg and sausage. Right away, enjoy or freeze in plastic wrap

Chocolate Melt Chaffles

Servings: 4
Cooking Time: 36 Minutes

Ingredients:
- For the chaffles:
- 2 eggs, beaten
- ¼ cup finely grated Gruyere cheese
- 2 tbsp heavy cream
- 1 tbsp coconut flour
- 2 tbsp cream cheese, softened
- 3 tbsp unsweetened cocoa powder
- 2 tsp vanilla extract
- A pinch of salt
- For the chocolate sauce:
- 1/3 cup + 1 tbsp heavy cream
- 1 ½ oz unsweetened baking chocolate, chopped
- 1 ½ tsp sugar-free maple syrup
- 1 ½ tsp vanilla extract

Directions:
1. For the chaffles:
2. Preheat the waffle iron.
3. In a medium bowl, mix all the ingredients for the chaffles.
4. Open the iron and add a quarter of the mixture. Close and cook until crispy, 7 minutes.
5. Transfer the chaffle to a plate and make 3 more with the remaining batter.
6. For the chocolate sauce:
7. Pour the heavy cream into saucepan and simmer over low heat, 3 minutes.
8. Turn the heat off and add the chocolate. Allow melting for a few minutes and stir until fully melted, 5 minutes.
9. Mix in the maple syrup and vanilla extract.
10. Assemble the chaffles in layers with the chocolate sauce sandwiched between each layer.
    Slice and serve immediately.

Nutrition Info:
Calories 172Fats 13.57gCarbs 6.65gNet Carbs 3.65gProtein 5.76g

Low Carb Chaffle Bowl

Servings: 1
Preparation time: 5 minutes
Nutritional Values: 150 kcal Calories | 17g Fat | 3g Carbs | 7g Proteins

Ingredients

- 1 whipped egg
- 1 scoop of keto meal chocolate
- 1 tbsp of almond flour
- 1/4 tsp of baking powder

Directions

1. Preheat then sprinkle the "Bowl Waffle Maker" with non-stick cooking oil

2. Break the egg in a little bowl. Whisk the egg

3. Add in the almond flour, keto meal and baking powder

4. Mix till the components completely come together

5. Put the material around 1 minute to 1.5 minute into the heated waffle maker. When you see steam come out of the maker, you'll realize it's nearly done

6. Utilize tongs to consider removing the hot chaffle bowl from the maker

7. Let it cool down and enjoy it

Pumpkin & Pecan Chaffle

Servings: 2
Cooking Time: 10 Minutes

Ingredients:

- 1 egg, beaten
- ½ cup mozzarella cheese, grated
- ½ teaspoon pumpkin spice
- 1 tablespoon pureed pumpkin
- 2 tablespoons almond flour
- 1 teaspoon sweetener
- 2 tablespoons pecans, chopped

Directions:

1. Turn on the waffle maker.
2. Beat the egg in a bowl.
3. Stir in the rest of the ingredients.
4. Pour half of the mixture into the device.
5. Seal the lid.
6. Cook for 5 minutes.
7. Remove the chaffle carefully.
8. Repeat the steps to make the second chaffle.

Nutrition Info:
Calories 210Total Fat 17 g Saturated Fat 10 g Cholesterol 110 mg Sodium
250 mg Potassium 570 mgTotal Carbohydrate 4.6 g Dietary Fiber 1.7 g
Protein 11 g Total Sugars 2 g

Spicy Jalapeno & Bacon Chaffles

Servings:2
Cooking Time: 5 Minutes

Ingredients:

- 1 oz. cream cheese
- 1 large egg
- 1/2 cup cheddar cheese
- 2 tbsps. bacon bits
- 1/2 tbsp. jalapenos
- 1/4 tsp baking powder

Directions:

1. Switch on your waffle maker.
2. Grease your waffle maker with cooking spray and let it heat up.
3. Mix together egg and vanilla extract in a bowl first.
4. Add baking powder, jalapenos and bacon bites.
5. Add in cheese last and mix together.
6. Pour the chaffles batter intothe maker and cook the chaffles for about 2-3 minutesutes.
7. Once chaffles are cooked, remove from the maker.
8. Serve hot and enjoy!

Nutrition Info: Per Servings:
Protein: 24% 5kcal Fat: 70% 175 kcal Carbohydrates: 6% 15 kcal

Cheddar & Almond Flour Chaffles

Servings: 2
Cooking Time: 10 Minutes

Ingredients:

- 1 large organic egg, beaten
- ½ cup Cheddar cheese, shredded
- 2 tablespoons almond flour

Directions:

1. Preheat a mini waffle iron and then grease it.
2. In a bowl, place the egg, Cheddar cheese and almond flour and beat until well combined.
3. Place half of the mixture into preheated waffle iron and cook for about 5 minutes or until golden brown.
4. Repeat with the remaining mixture.
5. Serve warm.

Nutrition Info: Per Servings:
Calories: 195Net Carb: 1gFat: 15.Saturated Fat:
7gCarbohydrates: 1.8gDietary Fiber: 0.8g Sugar: 0.6gProtein: 10.2g

Keto Turkey Brie Cranberry Chaffle Sandwich

Servings: 1
Preparation time: 5 minutes
Nutritional values: 537 kcal Calories | 36 g Fat |
8.6 g Carbs | 44 g Proteins

Ingredients

- 1/2 cup grated mozzarella
- 1 medium beaten egg
- 2 tbsp of almond flour

Filling

- 2 slices of turkey
- 3 Slices Brie
- 2 tbsp chia cranberry jam

Directions

1. Turn your waffle maker on and grease it gently
2. Add the egg, mozzarella, and almond flour in a bowl. Combine until mixed
3. Spoon the mixture into the waffle maker. If you want a small waffle maker, spoon half the batter in at a time)
4. Close the lid and cook until golden and firm for 5 minutes
5. Use tongs to remove the cooked waffles and set aside
6. Place the turkey, brie, and cranberry on a cutting board and layer on chaffle. Put the layers together with your choice
7. Place on top of the other chaffle and sliced in half
8. If you just want a warm sandwich, then heat it up for 20 seconds in the microwave

Simple& Beginner Chaffle

Servings:2
Cooking Time: 5 Minutes

Ingredients:

- 1 large egg
- 1/2 cup mozzarella cheese, shredded
- Cooking spray

Directions:

1. Switch on your waffle maker.
2. Beat the egg with a fork in a small mixing bowl.
3. Once the egg is beaten, add the mozzarella and mix well.
4. Spray the waffle makerwith cooking spray.
5. Pour the chaffles mixture in a preheated waffle maker and let it cook for about 2-3 minutes.
6. Once the chaffles are cooked, carefully remove them from the maker and cook the remaining batter.
7. Serve hot with coffee and enjoy!

Nutrition Info: Per Servings:
Protein: 36% 42 kcal Fat: 60% 71 kcal Carbohydrates: 4% 5 kcal

Arby's Chaffle

Servings: 2-3
Preparation time: 15 minutes
Nutritional Values: 386 kcal Calories | 20 g Fat |
8 g Carbs | 40 g Proteins

Ingredients
For beef:

- 1/2 cup of beef broth

  4 oz of deli roast beef, thinly sliced

-

For chaffle bun:
- 1 beaten egg
- 1 tsp of coconut flour
- 1/4 tsp of baking powder
- 1/2 cup of mozzarella, finely sliced

Arby's sauce-low carb:

- 1 tbsp of ketchup, sugar-free
- 2 tsp of salad dressing, Italian
- 1/4 tsp of Worcestershire sauce
- 1/4 tsp of chopped pepper

Directions
For beef:

- ✓ Add the broth of beef to a pan and take it to a boiling point. Include the beef in it and cook over low to warm the beef for five min. Cover it D and put aside when the chaffle is being prepared

For chaffle:

- ✓ Switch on to preheat your waffle maker
- ✓ Mix the coconut flour, egg as well as baking powder together. Then add the mozzarella in, and mix
- ✓ In waffle iron, pour half of the mixture. Lock the waffle machine and cook for three minutes. Take the waffle out and proceed with batter left over

For Arby's sauce:

    1. Mix all ingredients together to make the Arby's sauce

To assemble:

    ✓ Put the beef on one of the chaffles as well as drizzle it with Arby's sauce. Put the second chaffle over it

    ✓ Eat immediately

Notes

    • When preparing an onion bun, scatter over the chaffles the finely chopped dried onion.

        If you are an Arby sauce eater, you will need to double the recipe of sauce!

Keto Wonder-Bread Chaffle Sandwich

Serving: 2
Preparation time: 10 minutes
Nutritional values: 208 kcal Calories | 17.4g Fat |
2.1g Carbs | 10.3g Proteins

Ingredients for wonder-bread chaffle

- 2 eggs white
- 2 tbsp of almond flour
- 1 tbsp mayonnaise
- 1 tsp of water
- 1/4 tsp baking powder
- 1 pinch salt

Ingredients for sandwich elements

- 2 tbsp mayonnaise
- 1-piece deli ham
- 1 slice deli turkey
- 1 slice of cheese cheddar
- 1 tomato slice
- 1 leaf green leaf lettuce

Directions

1. Preheat the maker. Mix all the ingredients of the wonder-bread chaffle in a tiny bowl. White bread chaffle components combined together in a large bowl
2. Place 1/2 the batter into the waffle maker and cook for about 3 to 5 minutes until finished
3. Wonder-bread chaffle batter in a little waffle-maker
4. Remove the waffle when cooking has been completed. Repeat for the batter remaining
5. Made keto sandwich bread in a waffle maker
6. Place mayonnaise on one side of each bread chaffle sandwich. Place in green leaf, tomato and cold cuts

Asian Cauliflower Chaffles

Servings: 4

Cooking Time: 28 Minutes

Ingredients:

- For the chaffles:
- 1 cup cauliflower rice, steamed
- 1 large egg, beaten
- Salt and freshly ground black pepper to taste
- 1 cup finely grated Parmesan cheese
- 1 tsp sesame seeds
- ¼ cup chopped fresh scallions
- For the dipping sauce:
- 3 tbsp coconut aminos
- 1 ½ tbsp plain vinegar
- 1 tsp fresh ginger puree
- 1 tsp fresh garlic paste
- 3 tbsp sesame oil
- 1 tsp fish sauce
- 1 tsp red chili flakes

Directions:
1. Preheat the waffle iron.
2. In a medium bowl, mix the cauliflower rice, egg, salt, black pepper, and Parmesan cheese.
3. Open the iron and add a quarter of the mixture. Close and cook until crispy, 7 minutes.
4. Transfer the chaffle to a plate and make 3 more chaffles in the same manner.
5. Meanwhile, make the dipping sauce.
6. In a medium bowl, mix all the ingredients for the dipping sauce.
7. Plate the chaffles, garnish with the sesame seeds and scallions and serve with the dipping sauce.

Nutrition Info:
Calories 231Fats 188gCarbs 6.32gNet Carbs 5.42gProtein 9.66g

Egg-free Almond Flour Chaffles

Servings: 2
Cooking Time: 10 Minutes

Ingredients:

- 2 tablespoons cream cheese, softened
- 1 cup mozzarella cheese, shredded
- 2 tablespoons almond flour
- 1 teaspoon organic baking powder

Directions:

1. Preheat a mini waffle iron and then grease it.
2. In a medium bowl, place all ingredients and with a fork, mix until well combined.
3. Place half of the mixture into preheated waffle iron and cook for about 4-5 minutes or until golden brown.
4. Repeat with the remaining mixture.
5. Serve warm.

Nutrition Info: Per Servings:
Calories: 77Net Carb: 2.4gFat: 9.8g Saturated Fat:
4gCarbohydrates: 3.2gDietary Fiber: 0.8g Sugar: 0.3gProtein: 4.8g

Keto Chaffle Cuban Sandwich

Servings: 1-2
Preparation time: 10 minutes
Nutritional values: 522 kcal Calories | 33 g Fat |
4 g Carbs | 46 g Proteins

Ingredients

- 1 large egg
- 1 tbsp of almond flour
- 1 tbsp of Greek full-fat yogurt
- 1/8 tsp baking powder
- 1/4 cup swiss cheese crushed

For filling the sandwich

- 3 ounces roast pork
- 2 once deli ham
- 1 slice of Swiss cheese
- Chips of 3 to 5 pickles, sliced
- 1/2 tbsp Dijon mustard

Directions

1. Preheat your waffle iron
2. In a small bowl, mix the egg, yogurt, almond flour and baking powder together
3. Scatter one fourth of the Swiss shredded straight onto the hot waffle iron. Cover with half of the mixture of egg, then apply 1/4 more Swiss on it. Cover the iron and cook until light brown and crunchy for 3-5 minutes
4. Repeat the same procedure with the ingredients left behind
5. For the fillings in sandwich
6. In a small microwaveable dish, place the pork, Swiss cheese slice and ham in order. Microwave the cheese for 40 to 50 sec, before it melts
7. Cover with the mustard on the inner part of one chaffle, then finish with pickles. Reverse the bowl, so the molten Swiss hits the pickles on top of the chaffle. Put the chaffle at bottom on the roast pork & reverse the sandwich to keep the side of pork below and the side of mustard up

Keto Reuben Sandwich Chaffle

Servings: 1
Preparation time: 6 minutes
Nutritional values: 605 kcal Calories | 43.8 g Fat |
6.8 g Carbs | 45.1 g Proteins

Ingredients:
- 1 egg
- 1/2 cup mozzarella cheese
- 2 tbsp of flour (almond)
- 2 tbsp of low carbohydrate thousand island dressing
- 1/4 tsp baking powder
- 1/4 tsp of seeds of caraway
- 2 corned beef slices
- 1 Swiss cheese slice
- 2 tbsp of sauerkraut

Directions
1. set the temperature to the mid-high heat of the waffle maker

2. In a bowl, mix together the egg, mozzarella, almond flour, a tbsp of low carb dressing seeds of caraway as well as baking powder

3. Place the chaffle batter into the waffle maker center. Shut the waffle machine and let it be cooked for 5 to 7 min or till lightly browned and crisp is perfect. If a mini waffle maker is used, just spill half the mixture over the waffle machine. Two chaffles (mini) will be produced from this recipe

4. Take chaffle out from the waffle machine. If you are using a mini waffle machine, repeat for the residual batter

5. Place the corned beef on a sheet of parchment, and cover with a Swiss cheese slice. Heat for 20 to 30 sec in the oven, before the cheese begins to melt. Take off from the microwave. Place on each chaffle the remaining tbsp of low carbohydrate thousand island sauce spread the Swiss cheese and hot corned beef, and finish with sauerkraut as well as other chaffle

Keto Chocolate Fudge Chaffle

Servings: 2
Cooking Time: 14 Minutes

Ingredients:

- 1 egg, beaten
- ¼ cup finely grated Gruyere cheese
- 2 tbsp unsweetened cocoa powder
- ¼ tsp baking powder
- ¼ tsp vanilla extract
- 2 tbsp erythritol
- 1 tsp almond flour
- 1 tsp heavy whipping cream
- A pinch of salt

Directions:

1. Preheat the waffle iron.
2. Add all the ingredients to a medium bowl and mix well.
3. Open the iron and add half of the mixture. Close and cook until golden brown and crispy, 7 minutes.
4. Remove the chaffle onto a plate and make another with the remaining batter.
5. Cut each chaffle into wedges and serve after.

Nutrition Info: Per Servings:
Calories 173Fats 13.08gCarbs 3.98gNet Carbs 2.28gProtein 12.27g

Broccoli & Cheese Chaffle

Servings: 2
Cooking Time: 8 Minutes

Ingredients:

- ¼ cup broccoli florets
- 1 egg, beaten
- 1 tablespoon almond flour
- ¼ teaspoon garlic powder
- ½ cup cheddar cheese

Directions:

1. Preheat your waffle maker.
2. Add the broccoli to the food processor.
3. Pulse until chopped.
4. Add to a bowl.
5. Stir in the egg and the rest of the ingredients.
6. Mix well.
7. Pour half of the batter to the waffle maker.
8. Cover and cook for 4 minutes.
9. Repeat procedure to make the next chaffle.

Nutrition Info:

Calories 170Total Fat 13 g Saturated Fat 7 g Cholesterol 112 mg Sodium 211 mg Potassium 94 mgTotal Carbohydrate 2 g Dietary Fiber 1 g Protein 11 g Total Sugars 1 g

Cream Cheese Chaffle With Lemon Curd

Servings: 2
Preparation Time: 5 min
Nutritional Values: 302 kcal Calories | 24 g Fat | g Carbs | 15 g Proteins

Ingredients

- 1 batch keto lemon curd
- 3 large eggs
- 4 oz of softened cream cheese
- 1 tbsp of low carbohydrate sweetener
- 1 tsp of vanilla extract
- 3/4 cup of shredded mozzarella cheese
- 3 tbsp of coconut flour
- 1 tsp of baking powder
- 1/3 tsp of salt
- keto whipped cream, homemade (additional and optional)

Directions

1. Make lemon curd, and then let chill in the fridge
2. In the meantime, warm up your waffle maker and oil it like you usually do
3. Put baking powder, coconut flour and salt in a little bowl. Mix together and put away
4. Put the eggs, sweetener, vanilla and cream cheese into a large bowl. Beat till frothy by using a hand beater. You might have blocks of remaining cream cheese, so that's okay
5. Combine the egg mixture with the mozzarella cheese and keep beating
6. Put dry ingredients into the mixture and proceed to mix until well mixed
7. Put batter in the hot waffle maker and prepare a waffle as you do. Sometimes a few mins
8. Take away from waffle processor, coat with cooled lemon curd, then serve with optional whipped cream

Keto French Dip Chaffwich

Servings: 1-2
Preparation time: 10 minutes
Nutritional values: 444 kcal Calories | 26 g Fat | 6 g Carbs | 45 g Proteins

Ingredients

- 4 ounces of roasted beef
- 2 eggs (egg whites only)
- 2 tbsp almond flour
- 1 tbsp of sour cream
- 1-1/2 cup mozzarella
- 1/2 cup beef broth low in sodium

Directions

1. Whip the egg white till foamy, to make the chaffle. Include the almond flour and sour cream and mix properly. Add the cheese in

2. Heat up the mini waffle maker according to instructions from the manufacturer. Add half the batter when heated and cook for 7-10 mins once the chaffle is nicely browned and readily releases. Repeat with the batter left behind

3. In the meanwhile, heat the beef broth in a tiny pot or pan. Heat up the sliced beef, don't overcook it!

4. Put the processed beef on the chaffle to be assembled, top with cheese and serve sideways with the available broth

Zucchini Parmesan Chaffles

Servings: 2
Cooking Time: 14 Minutes

Ingredients:

- 1 cup shredded zucchini
- 1 egg, beaten
- ½ cup finely grated Parmesan cheese
- Salt and freshly ground black pepper to taste

Directions:

1. Preheat the waffle iron.
2. Put all the ingredients in a medium bowl and mix well.
3. Open the iron and add half of the mixture. Close and cook until crispy, 7 minutes.
4. Remove the chaffle onto a plate and make another with the remaining mixture.
5. Cut each chaffle into wedges and serve afterward.

Nutrition Info: Per Servings:
Calories 138Fats 9.07gCarbs 3.81gNet Carbs 3.71gProtein 10.02g

Keto Ham And Cheese Chaffle Sandwich

Servings: 1
Preparation Time: 15 Minutes
Nutritional Values: 733 Kcal Calories | 57.1g Fat | 8.4g Carbs | 45.8g Proteins

Ingredients

- 1 egg, should be large
- 1/2 cup crushed cheddar, mozzarella or any
- grated cheese 1/4 cup almond flour.
- 1/4 tsp gluten-free baking powder
- 2 ham slices
- 57g - 2 slices of cheese
- 4 - 60g tomato slices
- 15g - 2 small leaves of lettuce
- Optional: 1 or 2 tbsp of cream cheese, butter, or mayonnaise.

Directions

1. Start making the chaffles as per the directions. Either you can create 2 standard chaffles, or 3 thinner ones
2. Let the chaffles all cool down. They will be soft when hot but will crisp when getting colder
3. Fill with ham, cheese, lettuce and tomato croutons. Optionally, before filling, you can add 1 to 2 spoonsful of cream cheese and spread it over the chaffles
4. Immediately enjoy or place the chaffles in a sealed container for up to 3 days at room temperature or in the refrigerator for up to a week. Freeze for up to 3 months, for longer storage. The jar would maintainthe soft texture, but if you want crispy, you should leave them untouched

Fudgy Chocolate Desert Chaffles

Servings: 4
Preparation time: 5 minutes
Nutritional Values: 83 kcal Calories | 5.4 g Fat | 3 g Carbs | 6.1 g Proteins

Ingredients

- 2 eggs, large
- 2 tbsp whipping cream, heavy
- 4 tbsp of crushed mozzarella cheese
- 1 tbsp of dark cacao
- 2 tsp of coconut flour
- 1/2 tsp of baking powder (gluten-free)
- 1/2 tsp of vanilla extract (gluten-free)
- 1/4 tsp of stevia powder
- A pinch of salt

Directions

1. Get your waffle maker preheated. Sprinkle gently with cooking spray (high-heat)

2. Whip the eggs as well as cream in a bowl. Insert the rest of the ingredients, then mix to blend

3. When you have heated the waffle iron, spread the mixture in the fillable parts, making sure not to overload the area of the plate

4. Shut the cover to cook. There might be some steam coming from the edges as the chaffles cook, and the cover will rise gradually as they cook

5. Both are indications that tasty chaffles are on the way

6. Cook them for 3 to 5 min till the indicator light is turned green, or when the upper cover moves easily as well as the chaffles appear fluffy and brownish. Carefully remove the chaffles from the waffle maker, because it is really hot

7. Repeat 3 & 4 steps until the residual batter is used

8. Put in the plate, then serve as a low-carb snack with whipped cream & fruit, or (sugar-free) ice cream

Chaffled Brownie Sundae

Servings: 4
Cooking Time: 30 Minutes

Ingredients:

- For the chaffles:
- 2 eggs, beaten
- 1 tbsp unsweetened cocoa powder
- 1 tbsp erythritol
- 1 cup finely grated mozzarella cheese
- For the topping:
- 3 tbsp unsweetened chocolate, chopped
- 3 tbsp unsalted butter
- ½ cup swerve sugar
- Low-carb ice cream for topping
- 1 cup whipped cream for topping
- 3 tbsp sugar-free caramel sauce

Directions:

1. For the chaffles:
2. Preheat the waffle iron.
3. Meanwhile, in a medium bowl, mix all the ingredients for the chaffles.
4. Open the iron, pour in a quarter of the mixture, cover, and cook until crispy, 7 minutes.
5. Remove the chaffle onto a plate and make 3 more with the remaining batter.
6. Plate and set aside.
7. For the topping:
8. Meanwhile, melt the chocolate and butter in a medium saucepan with occasional stirring, 2 minutes.
9. To Servings:
10. Divide the chaffles into wedges and top with the ice cream, whipped cream, and swirl the chocolate sauce and caramel sauce on top.
11. Serve immediately.

Nutrition Info:
Calories 165Fats 11.39gCarbs 3.81gNet Carbs 2.91gProtein 79g

Keto chaffle sandwich recipes

Chicken Jalapeño Chaffles

Servings: 2
Cooking Time: 14 Minutes

Ingredients:

- 1/8 cup finely grated Parmesan cheese
- ¼ cup finely grated cheddar cheese
- 1 egg, beaten
- ½ cup cooked chicken breasts, diced
- 1 small jalapeño pepper, deseeded and minced
- 1/8 tsp garlic powder
- 1/8 tsp onion powder
- 1 tsp cream cheese, softened

Directions:
1. Preheat the waffle iron.
2. In a medium bowl, mix all the ingredients until adequately combined.
3. Open the iron and add half of the mixture. Close and cook until crispy, 7 minutes.
4. Transfer the chaffle to a plate and make a second chaffle in the same manner.
5. Allow cooling and serve afterward.

Nutrition Info:
Calories 201Fats 11.49gCarbs 3.7Net Carbs 3.36gProtein 20.11g

Keto Red Velvet Chaffle Cake

Servings: *1*
Preparation Time: *20 Minutes*
Nutritional Values: *291 kcal Calories | 30 g Fat | 6 g Carbs | 9 g Proteins*

Ingredients

- 2 tbsp of cocoa, Dutch processed
- 2 tbsp Monk Fruit sweetener
- 1 egg
- 2 drops of food color super red, it's optional
- 1/4 tsp of baking powder
- 1 tbsp of whipping cream (heavy)

For Frosting

- 2 tbsp of Monk Fruit sweetener
- 2 tbsp of softened cream cheese at room temp
- 1/4 tsp of clear vanilla

Directions

1. Whisk the egg in a little bowl
2. Transfer the rest of the ingredients and blend until the mixture is creamy and smooth
3. Place half the mixture into a waffle maker then cook for about 2 1/2–3 minutes till it is cooked completely
4. Put the cream cheese, sweetener and vanilla in a separate, little bowl. Blend the frosting till all is fully mixed
5. Apply the frosting over the chaffle cake after bringing it to room temperature exactly

Pumpkin-cinnamon Churro Sticks

Servings: 2
Cooking Time: 14 Minutes

Ingredients:

- 3 tbsp coconut flour
- ¼ cup pumpkin puree
- 1 egg, beaten
- ½ cup finely grated mozzarella cheese
- 2 tbsp sugar-free maple syrup + more for serving
- 1 tsp baking powder
- 1 tsp vanilla extract
- ½ tsp pumpkin spice seasoning
- 1/8 tsp salt
- 1 tbsp cinnamon powder

Directions:

1. Preheat the waffle iron.
2. Mix all the ingredients in a medium bowl until well combined.
3. Open the iron and add half of the mixture. Close and cook until golden brown and crispy, 7 minutes.
4. Remove the chaffle onto a plate and make 1 more with the remaining batter.
5. Cut each chaffle into sticks, drizzle the top with more maple syrup and serve after.

Nutrition Info: Per Servings:

Calories 219Fats 9.72gCarbs 8.gNet Carbs 4.34gProtein 25.27g

Low-Carb Chocolate Chip Vanilla Chaffles

Servings: 1-2
Preparation Time: 1 min
Nutrition Facts: 386 kcal calories | 28.1 g Fat | 8.2 g Carbs | 24.7 g Proteins

Ingredients

- 1/2 cup of pre-shredded or grated mozzarella
- 1 egg
- 1 tbsp granulated sugar substitute
- 1 tsp of vanilla extract
- 2 tbsp of almond meal or flour
- 1 tbsp of chocolate chips

Directions

1. Integrate your chosen components together in a bowl
2. Preheat your mini waffle processor. When it becomes hot, sprinkle with olive oil & spill half the mixture into the waffle maker
3. Cook for 2 to 4 min and then put it out and repeat
4. You must be capable of making two mini-chaffles each recipe
5. Topping, serve, as well as celebrate

Sharp Cheddar Chaffles

Servings: 2
Cooking Time: 10 Minutes

Ingredients:

- 1 organic egg, beaten
- ½ cup sharp Cheddar cheese, shredded

Directions:

1. Preheat a mini waffle iron and then grease it.
2. In a small bowl, place the egg and cheese and stir to combine.
3. Place half of the mixture into preheated waffle iron and cook for about 5 minutes or until golden brown.
4. Repeat with the remaining mixture.
5. Serve warm.

Nutrition Info: Per Servings:
Calories: 145Net Carb: 0.5gFat: 11.Saturated Fat: 6.6gCarbohydrates: 0.5gDietary Fiber: 0g Sugar: 0.3gProtein: 9.8g

Sweet Chaffle Recipes

Keto Breakfast Chaffle Sandwich

Servings: 1
Preparation time: 10 minutes
Nutritional values: 346.6 kcal Calories | 27.9 g Fat | 1.2g Carbs | 22.5g Proteins

Ingredients

- 1 Large egg
- 1\2 of shredded cheese (cheddar)
- 2 tsp mayonnaise
- 1-2 pcs of bacon
- 1 egg

Directions

1. Heat up the mini waffle iron
2. Add the shredded cheese and the egg in a little bowl, whereas the waffle iron is heating
3. Pour half the batter onto the waffle maker and cook 3-4 minutes or until you want waffles close
4. Cook the bacon in a small saucepan until crispy nicely browned, then set aside
5. Cook the egg to ideal doneness using the same tiny saucepan, add sea salt and pepper to fit
6. Put in the mayonnaise, bacon, and egg. to the chaffle

Club Sandwich Chaffle

Servings: *1-2*
Preparation time: *10 minutes*
Nutritional Values: *1078 kcal Calories | 86 g Fat | 12 g Carbs | 66 g Proteins*

Ingredients

- 2 batches of chaffle simple recipe
- 2 strips of sugar-free bacon
- 2 Oz free of sugar sliced deli turkey
- 2 Oz sugar-free sliced deli ham
- 1 slice of cheese (cheddar)
- 1 tomato slice
- 3 lettuce leaves
- 1 tbsp mayonnaise free of sugar

Directions

1. *Cook the chaffles and put aside, as instructed. Cover to keep warm*

2. *Cook the Bacon using your chosen (oven/microwave/stovetop) cooking process. By putting them in the microwave, sealed, keep it basic for around 2-3 minutes (based on how crispy you want it and the brand). When cooked, move to a lined sheet of paper towel*

3. *Make your sandwich, start the club sandwich with one chaffle and complete with the tomato and the lettuce. Add the other chaffle and the cheese, ham, turkey and Bacon on top. Smear the final chaffle with mayo, then put it on top of the sandwich*

4. *Enjoy it right away*

KETO CHAFFLE PLUS OMAD SANDWICH

Servings: *1*
Preparation time: *5 minutes*
Nutritional Values:

WAFFLE:
458 kcal Calories | 33.4g Fat | 3.5g Carbs | 26.7g Proteins

SANDWICH:
1168 kcal Calories | 84.2g Fat | 8.7g Carbs | 99.4g Proteins

Ingredients

WAFFLE
- 3/4 cup (75 g) shredded cheese (any of your choice)
- 1 medium-sized egg
- 1 tsp husk of psyllium
- salt / pepper
- Hot sauce (Optional)

SANDWICH
- 4 bacon strips
- 4 ham slices
- 4 prosciutto slices
- 5-6 salami slices
- 5-6 small pepperoni slices
- Mustard
- Mayonnaise

Directions
1. Whisk the egg, cheese, salt, pepper, psyllium husk together in a bowl, and additional hot sauce
2. Keep the waffle maker to heat until the batter is uniformly poured into the waffle pan
3. Cook 2-3 minutes or more based on how crispy you like it to be
4. Carry it out and eat the sandwich as is or top with delicious ingredients, fat-filled dinner

Cheesy Chaffle Sandwich's With Avocado And Bacon

Servings: *1-2*
Preparation time: *25 minutes*
Nutritional Values: *259 kcal Calories | 20.1 g Fat | 6.8 g Carbs | 14 g Proteins*

Ingredients

- 10 eggs
- 1 1/2 cups of shredded cheddar cheese
- 2 center cut slices of bacon, cooked and
- crumbled 1⁄2 tsp of ground pepper
- 2 small, sliced avocados
- 2 little tomatoes, in slices
- 4 large lettuce leaves, torn into 3 "parts

Directions

1. In a large bowl, whisk the eggs until smooth. Stir in cheese and chopped bacon and pepper

2. Preheat a 7-inch (not Belgian) round waffle iron; top it with cooking spray. Pour approximately 2/3 cup of the beaten egg into the waffle iron. Cook 4 to 5 minutes till the eggs are set and light golden brown. Repeat with cooking spray and the residual mixture of eggs (making a total of 4 chaffles)

3. Split each of the chaffles into pieces. Top half of the quarters even with slices of avocado, tomato slices and lettuce. Also, top the remaining quarters of the chaffle

Mozzarellas & Psyllium Husk Chaffles

Servings: 2
Cooking Time: 8 Minutes

Ingredients:

- ½ cup Mozzarella cheese, shredded
- 1 large organic egg, beaten
- 2 tablespoons blanched almond flour
- ½ teaspoon Psyllium husk powder
- ¼ teaspoon organic baking powder

Directions:

Preheat a mini waffle iron and then grease it.

In a bowl, place all the ingredients and beat until well combined.

Place half of the mixture into preheated waffle iron and cook for about 4 minutes or until golden brown.

Repeat with the remaining mixture.

Serve warm.

Nutrition Info: Per Servings:
Calories: 101Net Carb: 1.Fat: 7.1g Saturated Fat: 1.8gCarbohydrates: 2.9gDietary Fiber: 1.3g Sugar: 0.2gProtein: 6.7g

Keto Peanut Butter Cup Chaffle

Servings: 2
Preparation Time: 2 minutes
Nutritional Value: 264 kcal Calories | 21.6 g Fat | 7.25 g Carbs | 9.45 g Proteins

Ingredients
For Chaffle

- 1 egg
- 1 tbsp of heavy cream
- 1 tbsp of unsweetened cocoa
- 1 tbsp of Lakanto powdered sugar substitute
- 1 tsp of coconut flour
- 1/2 tsp of vanilla extract
- ½ tsp of cake batter flavoring
- 1/4 tsp of baking powder

For filling of peanut butter

- 3 tbsp of peanut butter, all natural
- 2 tsp of Lakanto powdered sugar substitute

  2 tbsp of heavy cream

Instructions

Combine all the ingredients for the chaffle in a little bowl

Place half the batter into the waffle iron center. Let it cook for 3-5 minutes

Cautiously remove, then repeat for next chaffle. Let the chaffles stay for a couple of minutes, so they become crispy

For the filling, combine all components together and then spread it between the chaffles

Chocolate & Almond Chaffle

Servings: 3
Cooking Time: 12 Minutes

Ingredients:

- 1 egg
- ¼ cup mozzarella cheese, shredded
- 1 oz. cream cheese
- 2 teaspoons sweetener
- 1 teaspoon vanilla
- 2 tablespoons cocoa powder
- 1 teaspoon baking powder
- 2 tablespoons almonds, chopped
- 4 tablespoons almond flour

Directions:

Blend all the ingredients in a bowl while the waffle maker is preheating.

Pour some of the mixture into the waffle maker.

Close and cook for 4 minutes.

Transfer the chaffle to a plate. Let cool for 2 minutes.

Repeat steps using the remaining mixture.

Nutrition Info:

Calories 1 Total Fat 13.1g Saturated Fat 5g Cholesterol 99mg Sodium 99mg
Potassium 481mg Total Carbohydrate 9.1g Dietary Fiber 3.8g Protein 7.8g
Total Sugars 0.8g

Low Carb Keto Chaffle Sandwich

Servings: 1-2
Preparation time: 10 minutes
Nutritional Values: 320 kcal Calories | 24g Fat | 5g Carbs | 21g Proteins

Ingredients

- 10 tbsp parmesan shredded cheese
- 1 cup of mozzarella shredded
- 2 slices of bacon (chopped)
- 1/4 tsp dry oregano
- 1 heaping tbsp of birch benders pancake mix (can be substituted for gf flour or desired mixture)
- 2 chickens 2 eggs
- Mayo
- 2 tiny or 1 large, thinly cut tomato
- Salt and pepper to fit

Directions

Put the egg, oregano, mozzarella cheese pancake mixture and salt and pepper into a food processor. Pulse blend until complete. Should just take a few steps

Add bacon and pulse in the mixture until bacon is uniformly dispersed

Put 1 tbsp of parmesan on the waffle maker bottom. 1 Heaping waffle mixture spoonful and 1 tbsp parmesan on top. Cover the waffle maker and finish cooking till golden brown. Repeat until the entire mix is used. It can yield about five mini waffles

Apply mayo on the waffle side. Add sliced tomato, salt and pepper to taste. Attach 2nd waffle to the end, and you've got a tomato sammie chaffle

Keto Snickerdoodle Chaffles

Servings: 1
Preparation time: 15 minutes
Nutritional values: 186 kcal Calories | 15.5 g Fat | 3.2 g Carbs | 8.4 g Proteins

Ingredients
Waffles:

- 1 egg, large
- 1/2 cup of crushed mozzarella (low-moisture)
- 1/4 cup of almond flour
- 1/8 tsp of baking powder, gluten-free
- 3 tbsp of low-carb granulated sweeteners like swerve or erythritol

Topping

- 1 1/2 tbsp of unsalted butter, melted
- 1 tsp of cinnamon
- 3 tbsp of low-carb granulated sweeteners like swerve or erythritol

Directions

For the waffles, measure all the ingredients. Preheat your waffle machine

You may either add all of the components in a medium bowl then mix them until incorporated or blend them together. Put the mozzarella, eggs, almond flour & baking powder in a food processor or blender for this

Insert the sweetener then mix in. Blending remains optional but strongly encouraged

To form 3 small chaffles, pour a third of the mixture into the preheated waffle maker

Cover the maker then cook for three to four mins. Keep a close eye on the mixture if it overflows

Lift the lid once ready, and allow it to cool down for a little bit. Using a spatula to move the chaffle softly onto a cooling tray

Repeat the procedure for the batter, which is remaining. When they're hot, the chaffles will be fluffy but would crisp up when they're finally chill

Easy Chaffle Sandwich

Servings: *1*
Preparation time: *5 minutes*
Nutritional values: *269 kcal Calories | 17g Fat | 8g Carbs | 20 g Proteins*

Ingredients

- 1 large egg
- 1/2 cup of mozzarella
- 1 tbsp (standard, gluten-free, almond or coconut flour)
- 1/2 tsp of baking powder
- 1 pinch salt

Directions

Coat nonstick cooking spray on the interior of a waffle maker. Preheat the waffle maker

Beat the egg in a little mixing bowl or cup. Mix the flour, baking powder, salt and combine properly

Stir in the scrambled cheese

Put the batter into the waffle iron. When using a mini-waffle machine, simply add in half of the mix

Lower with the cover. If the waffle maker has indicated the waffle is finished, raise the cover and transfer the waffle gently to a cooling rack. Use tongs to protect the fingertips from burning

Repeat this step until the amount of chaffles you want is reached

Open-Faced French Dip Keto Chaffle Sandwich

Servings: 1
Preparation time: 5 minutes
Nutritional values: 118 kcal Calories | 8 g Fat | 2 g Carbs | 9 g Proteins

Ingredients

- 1 egg white
- 1/4 cup, shredded (packed) mozzarella
- cheese 1/4 cup, shredded (packed)
- sharp cheddar cheese 3/4 tsp water
- 1 tsp of coconut flour
- 1/4 tsp baking powder

1 pinch salt

Directions

Preheat oven to 425 F. Plugin the wall of the Dash Mini Waffle Maker and graze gently until it is hot

Mix all the ingredients in a dish, then mix until combine

At the waffle maker, spoon 1/2 of the batter out and cover with a lid. Set a 4-minute timer, and do not raise the lid until the cooking period is complete. Preliminary lifting can cause separation of the chaffle keto sandwich recipe and stick to the waffle iron. Before you raise the lid, you have to let it cook the whole 4 minutes

Take the chaffle from the iron, then put aside. Repeat for the remaining of the chaffle batter on the same measures above

Position chaffles a few inches apart and cover a baking sheet with parchment paper

Add 1/4 to 1/3 cup slow cooker keto roast beef. Before applying to the top of the chaffle, be sure to remove the extra broth/gravy. (Recipes for the slow cooker)

Cover with a slice of deli cheese or sliced cheese. Both Swiss and the provolone are fantastic choices

Put on the oven's top rack for 5 minutes to allow the cheese to melt. If you want to bubble the cheese and start browning, set the oven to broil for 1 min. (Swiss cheese does not brown)

Enjoy open-faced and dipping with a tiny cup of beef broth

Strawberries And Cream Keto Chaffles

Servings: 1-2
Preparation Time: 25 min
Nutritional Values: 189 kcal Calories | 14.3 g Fat | 5.2 g Carbs | 10 g Proteins

Ingredients

- 3 ounces of cream cheese
- 2 cups of mozzarella cheese, shredded
- 2 eggs, whipped
- 1/2 cup of almond flour
- 2 tsp of baking powder
- Eight strawberries
- A cup of whipped cream i.e., canister- two tbsp per waffle
- 1 tbsp of confectioner's sweetener, swerve

Directions

Put the mozzarella and the cream cheese to a microwave bowl and then cook for 1 min. Mix properly, then proceed to the next stage, if all of the cheese is melted. Or else cook for another 30 seconds and then combine properly

Beat the eggs in some other bowl, then add baking powder, almond flour and 3 tbsp swerve sweetener

Combine the mixture of cream cheese with the mixture of almond flour then blend properly, now add in Two chopped strawberries. Put it in the fridge for 20 min

Meanwhile, cut the leftover strawberries and apply Swerve's one tablespoon. Mix properly and set it aside or cold

Then pull the batter out from the refrigerator, after 20 min. Heat up the waffle iron, then go on for that so, if it has to be greased

Pick 1/4 cup of mix and transfer to the hot iron, to the middle. Ensure the waffles are tiny so that they'll be easy to bring out from the waffle maker

Whenever it's prepared, move to a plate and then let it be cool before adding strawberries and whipped cream

Easy Double Chocolate Chaffles

Servings: 2-3
Preparation Time: 1 min
Nutritional Values: 215.8 kcal Calories | 15.7 g Fat | 9.9 g Carbs | 11.5 g Proteins

Ingredients

- ✓ 1/2 cup of pre-shredded or grated mozzarella
- ✓ egg
- ✓ tbsp granulated sugar substitute
- ✓ 1 tsp of vanilla extract
- ✓ 2 tbsp of almond meal or flour
- ✓ 1 tsp of chocolate chips
- ✓ 2 tbsp of unsweetened cocoa powder
- ✓ 1 tsp of cream, heavy or double

Directions

Integrate your chosen components together in a bowl

Preheat your mini waffle processor. When it becomes hot, sprinkle with olive oil & spill half the mixture into the waffle maker

Cook for 2 to 4 min and then put it out and repeat

You must be capable of making two mini-chaffles each recipe

Topping, serve, as well as celebrate

Blt Chaffle Sandwich

Servings: 2
Preparation time: 10 minutes
Nutritional values: 183 kcal Calories | 13.9 g Fat | 1.4 g Carbs | 10.8 g Proteins

Ingredients for chaffle

- 1/2 cup, shredded mozzarella
- 1 egg
- 1 tbsp of green onion, chopped
- 1/2 tsp Seasoning (Italian)

Ingredients for Sandwich

- Pre-cooked bacon
- Lettuce
- Tomato, in slices
- 1 tbs of mayo

Directions

1. Heat up the mini-waffle maker
   Whip the egg in a little bowl

   Add the cheese, seasonings and onion to blend. Mix until it's fully set in

   In the mini waffle maker, place half the batter and cook for 4 minutes

   If you want a crunchy crust, apply a teaspoon of grated cheese to the mini waffle iron before adding the batter for 30 seconds. Extra cheese will create the best crust on the outside

   Following the completion of the first chaffle, add the rest batter to the waffle maker and cook for 4 minutes

   Fill your sandwich with the mayo, Bacon, lettuce, and tomato

Garlic Bread Chaffle

Serving: 2
Preparation time: 5 minutes
Nutritional Value: 186 kcal Calories | 14 g Fat | 3 g Carbs| 10 g Proteins

Ingredients

- 1 large egg
- 1/2 cup of mozzarella, finely shredded
- 1 tsp of coconut flour
- ¼ tsp of baking powder
- 1/2 tsp of garlic powder
- 1 tbsp of melted butter
- 1/4 tsp of garlic salt
- 2 tbsp of Parmesan
- 1 tsp of finely chopped parsley

Directions

Plugin, to preheat your waffle maker. Set Oven temperature to 375F and preheat

In a mixing bowl, add the mozzarella, egg, coconut flour, garlic powder and baking powder and stir well to blend

Put half the batter in the waffle iron, then cook about 3 min or till the steam has ended. On a baking sheet, put the prepared chaffle

With the leftover batter of the chaffle, repeat the same steps

Mix garlic salt and butter together, then over the chaffles, brush it

Sprinkle the Parmesan on the chaffles

Put the pan, 5 min in the oven to the cheese to be melt

Scatter the parsley over it prior to serving

Notes

- The garlic salt renders them mildly salty-if you're watching salt, feel free to add in freshly chopped garlic or even garlic powder.

Keto Taco Chaffles

Servings: 3-4
Preparation time: 5 minutes
Nutritional Values:
258 kcal Calories | 19 g Fat | 4 g Carbs | 18 g Proteins

Ingredients

- 1 egg white
- 1/4 cup of shredded Monterey jack cheese,
- (packed firmly) 1/4 cup of shredded sharp
- cheddar cheese, (packed firmly) 3/4 tsp of water
- 1 tsp of coconut flour
- 1/4 tsp of baking powder
- 1/8 tsp of chili powder
- 1 pinch salt

Directions

Plugin the wall, the Mini Waffle Maker and lightly grease it once it is warm

Incorporate all the components in a bowl and mix well to combine them

Pour half of the mixture on the maker and then shut the lid

Setup a 4-min timer, and thus do not remove the cover till the cooking duration is finished

If you do so, the taco chaffle will appear like it is not set up completely, but it would

Before you open the lid, you get to just let it prepare the whole 4 min

Put the taco shell out from the iron as well as set aside. Repeat the same procedure for the remaining portion of the chaffle batter

Switch a muffin pan over and place the taco chaffle between cups to create a taco shell. Let to set it for a couple of minutes

Keto Blueberry Chaffle

Servings: 1-2
Preparation Time: 3 minutes
Nutritional Value: 116 kcal Calories | 8 g Fat | 3 g Carbs | 8 g Proteins

Ingredients

- 1 cup mozzarella cheese
- 2 tbsp of almond flour
- 1 tsp of baking powder
- 2 eggs
- 1 tsp of cinnamon
- 2 tsp of swerve
- 3 tbsp of blueberries

Directions

1. Preheat your waffle maker
2. Put the almond flour, mozzarella cheese, baking powder, cinnamon, eggs, swerve & blueberries into a mixing bowl. Stir properly enough that the ingredients blend well
3. Sprinkle non-stick spray on the waffle maker
4. Insert less than one fourth a cup of keto blueberry waffle mixture
5. Shut the lid, then for 3-5 min, cook the chaffle. Assess it at 3 min tosee whether it's brown & crispy. Whether it isn't or if it sticks to the waffle maker's top, shut the cover then cook for 1 to 2 min
6. Represent with a light sprinkling of swerve or keto syrup

Chaffles With Raspberry Syrup

Servings: 4
Cooking Time: 38 Minutes

Ingredients:

- For the chaffles:
- 1 egg, beaten
- ½ cup finely shredded cheddar cheese
- 1 tsp almond flour
- 1 tsp sour cream
- For the raspberry syrup:
- 1 cup fresh raspberries
- ¼ cup swerve sugar
- ¼ cup water
- 1 tsp vanilla extract

Directions:

For the chaffles:

Preheat the waffle iron.

Meanwhile, in a medium bowl, mix the egg, cheddar cheese, almond flour, and sour cream.

Open the iron, pour in half of the mixture, cover, and cook until crispy, 7 minutes.

Remove the chaffle onto a plate and make another with the remaining batter.

For the raspberry syrup:

Meanwhile, add the raspberries, swerve sugar, water, and vanilla extract to a medium pot. Set over low heat and cook until the raspberries soften and sugar becomes syrupy. Occasionally stir while mashing the raspberries as you go.

Turn the heat off when your desired consistency is achieved and set aside to cool.

Drizzle some syrup on the chaffles and enjoy when ready.

Nutrition Info:
Calories 105Fats 7.11gCarbs 4.31gNet Carbs 2.21gProtein 5.83g

Keto Chaffles Benedict

Servings: 2
Preparation time: 20 minutes
Nutritional values: 352 kcal Calories | 26 g Fat | 4 g Carbs | 26 g Proteins

Ingredients
For Chaffle
- 2 egg whites
- 2 tbsp of almond flour
- 1 tbsp of sour cream
- 1/2 cup of mozzarella cheese

For hollandaise
- 1/2 cup of butter, salted
- 4 yolks of eggs
- 2 tbsp of Lemon juice

For poached eggs
- 2 whole eggs
- 1 tbsp of white vinegar
- 3 oz of deli ham

Directions
1. Preparing the chaffle: Beat the white of egg till frothy, now add in the rest of the ingredients and blend

2. Preheating the Mini Waffle Machine, then insert half of the batter of the chaffle into that. Sprinkle non-stick spray onto the chaffle maker

3. Cook till it becomes golden brown, for around 7 minutes. Pull the chaffle out and repeat

4. To make the Hollandaise sauce: organize a dual boiler (a pot which best fits on top with such a heat-safe bowl). Add sufficient water to boil in the pot, but do not contact the bowl's bottom

5. Hollandaise cont.: In the microwave, heat up the butter to boil. Place the egg yolks in the double boiler bowl and put the pot to boil.

6. Transfer the heated butter into the bowl when boiling the pot

7. Hollandaise cont.: Beat nimbly heating the batter from the water under the bowl. Keep cooking till the pot water boils, the yolk-butter combination has thickened, as well as very extremely hot. Take the bowl out of the pot and insert the lemon juice. Set aside

8. To poach the egg: If required, add a little more water in the pot (you have sufficient to completely cover the egg) & take it to simmer. Put two tablespoons of white vinegar into the water. Drop an egg cautiously into the boiling water and cook it for 90 sec. Put it out using a slotted spoon

9. To assemble: heat up the chaffle for some minutes in a toaster. Topping the crispy, crunchy chaffle with a poached egg, two tablespoons of hollandaise sauce and half of the ham pieces

Keto Chaffle Blt Regular Sandwich

Servings: 2
Preparation time: 3 minutes
Nutritional Values: 238kcal Calories | 18 g Fat | 2 g Carbs | 17 g Proteins

Ingredients
For chaffles
- 1 egg
- 1/2 cup of shredded cheddar cheese

For sandwich

- 2 bacon strips
- 1-2 tomato slices
- 2–3 lettuce pieces
- 1 tbsp of mayonnaise

Directions

Preheat your waffle maker as instructed by the manufacturer

Mix the shredded cheese and egg together in a little mixing bowl. Mix until you have integrated well

Pour half of the mixture into the maker. Cook for three to four minutes, or till its light brown. Do the same with the batter's second half

Cook the bacon in a large saucepan on medium heat till it's crispy and switch as required. Remove onto paper towels to drain

Organize the sandwich with tomato, lettuce & mayonnaise. Celebrate it

Notes

- If you're using a waffle maker of large size, you might become capable of cooking the entire batter amount in one waffle. That would vary with your machine's size.

Cheddar Chicken & Broccoli Chaffle

Servings: 2
Preparation time: 2 minutes
Nutritional values: 58 kcal Calories| 1 g Fat | 1 g Carbs| 7 g Proteins

Ingredients

- 1/4 cup of diced cooked chicken
- 1/4 cup of chopped fresh broccoli
- Cheddar cheese, shredded
- 1 egg
- 1/4 tsp of garlic powder

Directions

1. Preheat your waffle maker
2. Combine the garlic powder, egg and cheddar cheese in a small bowl
3. Add the chicken & broccoli, then stir properly
4. In the waffle maker, put 1/2 of the batter then cook it for 4 min. Let them cook for a further 2 min if they're still a little uncooked. After this, cook the remaining mixture to prepare a second chaffle and finally cook the 3rd chaffle
5. Take it out from the pan after cooking and let it stay for two min
6. Dip it in sour cream, ranch dressing, or you may enjoy alone

Keto Cauliflower Chaffles Recipe

Servings: 1-2
Preparation time: 5 minutes
Nutritional values: 246 kcal Calories | 16 g Fat | 7 g Carbs | 20 g Proteins

Ingredients

- 1 cup of cauliflower, riced
- 1/4 tsp of garlic powder
- 1/4 tsp of black pepper, ground
- 1/2 tsp of Italian Seasoning
- 1/4 tsp of Kosher salt
- 1/2 cup of mozzarella cheese shredded, or Mexican blend
- cheese shredded 1 egg
- 1/2 cup of parmesan cheese, shredded

Directions

Combine all the ingredients and put them into a blender

In waffle maker, scatter 1/8 cup of parmesan cheese. Ensure the waffle iron bottom is covered

Pour the cauliflower batter into the waffle machine

Put another scattering of parmesan cheese on the mixture's top. Ensure the top of the waffle iron is covered

Cook it for 4 to 5 min, or till its crispy

Tends to make four mini chaffles or two full-size chaffles

Cinnamon Powder Chaffles

Servings:2

Cooking Time: 5 Minutes

Ingredients:

- ✓ 1 large egg
- ✓ 3/4 cup cheddar cheese, shredded
- ✓ 2 tbsps. coconut flour
- ✓ 1/2 tbsps. coconut oil melted
- ✓ 1 tsp. stevia
- ✓ 1/2 tsp cinnamon powder
- ✓ 1/2 tsp vanilla extract
- ✓ 1/2 tsp psyllium husk powder
- ✓ 1/4 tsp baking powder

Directions:

Switch on your waffle maker.

Grease your waffle maker with cooking spray and heat up on medium heat.

In a mixing bowl, beat egg withcoconut flour, oil, stevia, cinnamon powder, vanilla, husk powder, and baking powder.

Once the egg is beaten well, add in cheeseand mix again.

Pour half of the waffle batter into the middle of your waffle iron and close the lid.

Cook chaffles for about 2-3 minutesutes until crispy.

Once chaffles are cooked, carefully remove them from the maker.

Serve with keto hot chocolate and enjoy!

Nutrition Info: Per Servings:

Protein: 25% 62 kcal Fat: 72% 175 kcal Carbohydrates: 3% 7 kcal

Easy Chaffle With Keto Sausage Gravy

Serving: 2-3
Preparation Time: 5 Minutes
Nutritional Value: 212 kcal Calories | 17 g Fat | 3 g Carbs | 11 g Proteins

Ingredients
For Chaffle:

- 1 egg
- 1/2 cup of grated mozzarella cheese
- 1 Tsp of fine coconut flour
- 1 tsp of water
- 1/4 tsp of baking powder
- A Salt pinches

For Keto Sausage Gravy:

- 1/4 cup of browned breakfast sausage
- 3 tbsp of chicken broth
- 2 tbsp of whipping cream, heavy
- 2 tsp of softened cream cheese
- garlic powder dash
- Add pepper to your taste
- dash onion powder (not mandatory)

Directions

Insert your Waffle Maker into the wall, as well as heat it up. Lightly grease or utilize cooking spray

Merge all the chaffle ingredients in a little bowl and mix well enough to merge

Add half the batter into the maker, then shut down the lid as well as cook for about 4 min

To prepare the second chaffle, Put the chaffle out from the waffle maker & do perform the same process. To be crispy, set aside

For Keto Sausage Gravy

Make one lb. of breakfast drain and sausage. For this, reserve one-fourth of a cup

Tip: From the leftover sausage, start making sausage patties as well as keep 1/4 of a cup for this dish to brown.

If you are unfamiliar with the sausage for breakfast, its crumble, such as ground beef.

Clean the extra oil from the pan and insert 1/4 cup golden brown breakfast sausage as well as the remaining ingredients, continues stirring to a boil.

Reduce the heat to medium, & continue cooking with the cover off to start thickening for about 5 to 7 min. If you want it to be very thick, you should apply some Xanthan Gum, though if you're careful with that as well, the gravy of keto sausage can thicken. Then as it cools, it

would thicken much more.

Season with salt and pepper over the chaffles, to taste, and add a spoonful of keto sausage gravy.

Nut-Free Keto Cinnamon Roll Chaffles

Serving: 2
Preparation Time: 15 min
Nutritional Value: 195 kcal Calories | 15.1 g Fat | 31.5 g Carbs | 8.5 g Proteins

Ingredients
For Batter:

- ½ cup of mozzarella cheese, shredded
- 2 tbsp of sweetener, golden monk fruit
- 2 tbsp of no-sugar-added "sun butter"
- 1 egg
- 1 tbsp of coconut flour
- 2 tsp of cinnamon
- ¼ tsp of vanilla extract
- ⅛ tsp of baking powder

For Frosting:

- ¼ cup of powdered sweetener monk fruit
- 1 tbsp of cream cheese
- ¾ tbsp of melted butter
- ¼ tsp of vanilla extract or ⅛ tsp of maple extract
- 1 tbsp of coconut milk, unsweetened

For Coating:
- 1 tsp of cinnamon
- 1 tsp of sweetener golden monk fruit

Directions

Switch on the waffle iron as well as enable to preheat during batter & frosting preparation

Batter: Put all the batter's components together in a big mixing pot. Set the pot aside for 3-5 min to make the batter set

Frosting: Mix over sweetener powdered monk fruit, sugar, maple or vanilla extract and cream cheese into a separate little combining bowl till smooth

Put in coconut milk then stir again till all components are well mixed. Set it aside

Last steps: Brush preheated iron generously with non-stick cooking spray

Start dividing the chaffle mixture into 3 servings & spoon 1 portion into the waffle iron; when cooking, the batter spreads, leave a slight gap at the edges

Cook batter for around 2-4 minutes until the chaffle is lightly browned

Open the lid of the waffle iron and allow the chaffle to cool down in the waffle iron for around 30 sec, before cautiously separating the chaffle, with a fork, at the edges and shifting it to a tray

Sprinkle cinnamon & monk fruit flavoring coating on chaffles when hot. Once mildly cools down, drizzle frosting atop chaffles

Notes:

- **Sun Butter replacement:** If you do not have an allergy to the nuts, you could even replace in either (unsweetened) almond butter or (unsweetened) peanut butter besides Sun Butter at quite a 1:1 ratio.
- **Net Carbohydrates:** One chaffle has 3.4 g of net carbohydrates in it.
- **Fridge Storage:** In an airtight jar or freezing bag, place those keto chaffles inside the refrigerator & consume within 3 days.
- **Freezer Storage:** In a freezing bag or airtight jar, place these chaffles and use a baking parchment sheet to divide each waffle so that they do not stick around each other. Place for 2 months in your freezer.
- **Reheating frozen or refrigerated chaffles**: Use a toaster for reheating refrigerated chaffles, a preheated oven toaster, or a preheated microwave and heat until it is all cooked.

Zucchini Chaffles

Servings: 2
Preparation time: 10 minutes
Nutritional values: 194 kcal Calories | 13 g Fat | 4 g Carbs | 16 g Proteins

Ingredients

- 1 cup of grated zucchini
- 1 beaten egg
- 1/2 cup of parmesan cheese, shredded
- 1/4 cup of mozzarella cheese, shredded
- 1 tsp of dried basil, or maybe even 1/4 cup of chopped
- fresh basil, 3/4 tsp of divided Kosher salt
- 1/2 tsp of ground black pepper

Directions

1. Sprinkle on the zucchini approximately 1/4 teaspoon salt and then let it sit whilst collecting your ingredients. In a paper towel, wrap the zucchini before just using, then to force all the extra water out, squeeze it
2. Beat the egg in a little bowl. Combine the grated zucchini, basil, mozzarella, 1/2 tsp of salt, and pepper
3. Scatter 1-2 spoonful of chopped parmesan to coat the waffle iron base
4. Scatter 1/4 of the mixture. Using about 1-2 tsp of chopped parmesan to cover and shut the lid. Using enough for surface covering. Check out the video and see how
5. Based on the size of the waffle maker cause the zucchini chaffle to be cooked for 4-8 mins. Usually, it is pretty much done when the processor has stopped the steam cloud emits. Let it cook till it's golden brown, for the great outcome
6. Remove it and repeat the same with the next waffle
7. Makes two full-size chaffles as well as four small chaffles, in the Mini maker
8. These chaffles freeze excellently. Freeze these, then warm them up again in the toaster or in your fryer to gain back crispiness

Spinach & Artichoke Chicken Chaffle

Servings: 2
Preparation Time: 3 minutes
Nutritional Values: 172 kcal Calories | 13 g Fat | 3 g Carbs | 11 g Proteins

Ingredients

- 1/3 cup of diced chicken, cooked
- 1/3 cup of cooked chopped spinach
- 1/3 cup of chopped marinated artichokes
- 1/3 cup of mozzarella cheese, shredded
- 1 oz of cream cheese, softened
- 1/4 tsp of garlic powder
- 1 egg

Directions

Preheat your waffle maker

Mix the garlic powder, eggs and cream cheese as well as Mozzarella cheese together in a little bowl

Add the chicken and artichoke and spinach and combine well

In your mini waffle maker, put 1/3 of the batter then cook it for four minutes. Let them cook for a further 2 minutes if they're still a little undercooked. Then cook the remaining mixture to create a second chaffle and finally prepare the final chaffle

Take it out from the maker after cooking and then let stay for two min

Dip in sour cream, ranch dressing or celebrate alone

Garlic Chaffles

Servings:4

Cooking Time: 5 Minutes

Ingredients:

- 1/2 cup mozzarella cheese, shredded
- 1/3 cup cheddar cheese
- 1 large egg
- ½ tbsp. garlic powder
- 1/2 tsp Italian seasoning
- 1/4 tsp baking powder

Directions:

Switch on your waffle maker and lightly grease your waffle maker with a brush.

Beat the egg with garlic powder, Italian seasoning and baking powder in a small mixing bowl.

Add mozzarella cheese and cheddar cheese tothe egg mixture and mix well.

Pour half of the chaffles batter into the middle of your waffle iron and close the lid.

Cook chaffles for about 2-3 minutesutes until crispy.

Once cooked, remove chaffles from the maker.

Sprinkle garlic powder on top and enjoy!

Nutrition Info: Per Servings:

Protein: 32% 36 kcal Fat: 61% 69 kcal Carbohydrates: 7% 7 kcal

Cinnamon Roll Keto Chaffles

Servings: 1-3
Preparation Time: 5 minutes
Nutritional Value: 180 kcal Calories | 16 g Fat | 3 g Carbs | 7 g Proteins

Ingredients

- 1/2 cup of mozzarella cheese
- 1 tbsp of almond flour
- 1/4 tsp of baking powder
- 1 egg
- 1 tsp of cinnamon
- 1 tsp of Swerve, granulated

For Cinnamon roll swirl

- 1 tbsp of butter
- 1 tsp of cinnamon
- 2 tsp of swerve

For Cinnamon Roll Glaze

- 1 tbsp of butter
- 1 tbsp of cream cheese
- 1/4 tsp of vanilla extract
- 2 tsp of swerve

Directions

1. Insert your waffle maker into the plug to heat it up

2. Mix almond flour, mozzarella cheese, baking powder, 1 tsp of cinnamon as well as 1 tsp of granulated swerve and an egg in a small bowl, then set it aside

3. Add a tsp of cinnamon, 1 tbsp of butter, as well as 2 tsp of swerve sweetener to some other little bowl

4. Microwave it for 15 sec and combine well

5. Sprinkle the non-stick spray on the waffle maker, then pour 1/3 of the mixture to the maker. Float in 1/3 of the swerve, butter and cinnamon blend onto the upper part of it. Shut the maker and then let it cook for three or four minutes

6. When you complete making the first roll chaffle, start making the second one and after that, make the next

7. When the third chaffle is preparing, put 1 tbsp of butter in a medium bowl and 1 tbsp of cream cheese. Microwave it for 10 to 15 sec. Begin at 10, and when the cream cheese isn't really soft enough even to blend with the heat of butter, for an extra 5 seconds, heat it

8. Add the sweetener & vanilla extract to the cream cheese and butter, then combine well with a whisk

9. Drizzle on top of the chaffle with keto cream cheese glaze

Keto Oreo Chaffles

Servings: 2
Preparation Time: 15 min
Nutritional Value: 1381 kcal Calories | 146 g Fat | 14 g Carbs | 17 g Protein

Ingredients

- 1/2 cup of sugar-free Choco-chips
- 1/2 cup of butter
- 3 eggs
- 1/4 cup of Truvia, or even other sweeteners
- 1 tsp of vanilla extract

Cream-Cheese Frosting

- 4 oz. of butter, at room temperature
- 4 oz. of cream cheese, at room temperature
- 1/2 cup of swerve, powdered
- 1/4 cup of whipping cream (heavy)
- 1 tsp of vanilla extract

Directions

1. Melt chocolate and butter in a protected bowl in a microwave for around 1 min. Remove it and mix nicely

2. You ought to just use the heat throughout chocolate and butter to melt the many of the chunks. You've over-cooked the chocolate whether you microwave till it's melted all over

3. Then get a spoon, as well as start to mix. If necessary, then add 10 sec, but mix perfectly before you intend to do so

4. Put the eggs, vanilla and sweetener in a bowl and combine until light & frothy

5. In a gradual flow, pour the melted chocolate and butter into the bowl, then beat again till well absorbed

6. Place approximately 1/4 of the blend into Mini Waffle Maker, then cook for 7-8 min or when it becomes crispy

7. Make the frosting as they cook

8. Put all the ingredients of frosting in a food processor's bowl and begin to process till fluffy and smooth. To achieve the right texture, you might need to put some more milk

9. To make the Oreo Chaffle, gently scatter or pipe the frosting amongst two chaffles

10. Should create 2 Oreo Chaffles in full size, or 4 Oreo Chaffles in mini size

Tips

- Just let waffles cool down more until they have eaten and frosting. It will enable them to be crispy.
- To make the frosting, use the room temp butter and cream cheese.

Keto Caramelchaffle

Servings: 2
Preparation time: 10 Minutes
Nutritional Values: 189 kcal Calories | 18 g Fat | 2 g Carbs | 20 g Proteins

Ingredients
For the chaffles:

- 1 tbsp of Swerve sweetener
- 2 tbsp of almond flour
- 1 egg
- 1/2 tsp of vanilla extract
- 1⁄3 cup of mozzarella cheese, shredded

For the caramel sauce:

- 3 tbsp of unsalted butter
- 2 tbsp of swerve substitute of brown sugar
- 1/3 cups of whipping cream, heavy
- 1/2 tsp of vanilla extract

Directions
1. Let your waffle iron preheat
2. Put 3 tbsp butter as well as the 2 tbsp substitute of brown sugar together in a small pan or skillet over a moderate flame on the stove
3. Cook the sugar substitute blend and butter for 4 to 5 minutes till it starts to get brown (but not burn)
4. Insert the whipping cream in the blend, which is on the stove, as well as stir in very well. Cook the batter for ten minutes on a low boil
5. before the mixture thickens and also has caramel sauce color
6. Mix all together components for the chaffles in a bowl, whereas the caramel sauce melts
7. Put half of the batter of the chaffle into the hot waffle maker then cook for 3 to 5 minutes till you have achieved the target degree of doneness
8. Take out the first chaffle, then cook the other half mixture for another 3 to 5 min
9. Remove the final caramel sauce from the stove, and insert the vanilla extract. Let it cool a bit.
10. Put over the chaffles, the caramel sauce and eat

Dill Pickle Egg Salad Sandwiches

Servings: 2-3
Preparation time: 10 minutes
Nutritional Values: 465 kcal Calories | 35 g Fat | 7 g Carbs | 30 g Protein

Ingredients
For egg salad:

- 6 eggs, hard-boiled
- ½ cup of dill pickles, chopped
- 3 tbsp of mayonnaise
- 1 tbsp of yellow mustard, prepared
- 1 tbsp of dill pickle juice
- 1 tbsp of dill, fresh
- Salt & pepper, as per your taste

For chaffles:

- 3 beaten eggs
- 1 tbsp of coconut flour
- 3/4 tsp of baking powder
- 1 1/2 cups of mozzarella finely chopped

Directions
To prepare egg salad:

Peel the eggs and chop them into tiny chunks

Put the eggs and remaining components to bowl. Mix well enough to combine

Eat right away or keep firmly wrapped in the refrigerator for up to four days

To prepare the chaffles:

Switch on to preheat your waffle maker

Stir the coconut flour, eggs as well as baking powder together. Add in the mozzarella cheese to integrate

Pour only enough mixture to cover the waffle iron bottom and shut the waffle iron. Cook them for 3 min. Take out the waffle and continue with the remaining mixture till you have prepared six chaffles

To assemble:

Split the egg salad equally among three chaffles

Put the left chaffles on top of them and eat

Notes

- If you would like to use almond flour instead of coconut flour, raise the quantity to 3 tbsp.

Big Mac Chaffle

Servings: 2
Preparation time: 10 min
Nutritional Values: 831 kcal Calories | 56 g Fat | 8 g Carbs | 65 g Proteins

Ingredients
For cheeseburgers:

- 1/3 lb. of ground beef
- 1/2 tsp of garlic salt
- 2 pieces of American cheese

The Chaffles:

- 1 big egg
- 1/2 cup of mozzarella finely shredded
- 1/4 tsp of garlic salt

For Big Mac Sauce:

- 2 tsp of mayonnaise
- 1 tsp of ketchup
- 1 tsp of dill pickle relish
- splash vinegar as per your taste

To assemble:

- 2 tbsp of chopped lettuce
- 3 to 4 of dill pickles
- 2 tsp of finely chopped onion

Directions
Making the Burgers

Over a mid/high heat, heat the griddle

Split the beef into two spheres of similar size and put each, at about 6 inches away, on the griddle

Let them cook for around 1 minute

Using a tiny salad plate to push the beef balls tightly, to straight down to flatten. Scatter the garlic salt

Cook for 2 minutes, or when cooked half completely. Carefully turn the burgers, then spray lightly with the leftover garlic salt

Keep cooking for 2 min or till cooked completely

Put one cheese slice on each patty, then pile the patties onto a plate & set aside. Wrap in foil

To make the chaffles:

Heat and spray the waffle iron with non-stick cooking oil spray

Mix the cheese, egg and garlic salt together until well mixed

In waffle iron, insert half egg mixture then cook for 2 to 3 minutes. Place aside and replicate the step with batter left over

Making Big Mac Sauce:
1. Mix all items together

To organize burgers:

With stacked patties, chopped lettuce, onions, and pickle, top one chaffle

Scatter the Big Mac sauce on the other chaffle, then put sauce on the sandwich face down

Eat right away

Keto Chaffle Garlic Cheesy Bread Sticks

Servings: 3-4
Preparation time: 3 Minutes
Nutritional values: 74 kcal Calories | 6.5 g Fat | 0.9 g Carbs | 3.4 g Proteins

Ingredients

- 1 medium-sized egg
- 1/2 cup of grated mozzarella cheese
- 2 tbsp of almond flour
- 1/2 tsp of garlic powder
- 1/2 tsp of oregano
- 1/2 tsp of salt

For Topping

- 2 tbsp of unsalted softened butter
- 1/2 tsp of garlic powder
- 1/4 cup of grated mozzarella cheese

Directions

Turn the waffle maker on and grease it gently by using olive oil

In a mixing bowl, whisk the egg

Insert the almond flour, mozzarella, oregano, garlic powder as well as salt and combine properly

Pour the mixture into the waffle maker

Shut the cover and cook for about five min

Use tongs, pick the prepared waffles, then slice each waffle into 4 pieces

Put these sticks on such a tray and heat the grill before that

Combine the garlic powder and butter together and scatter on over sticks

Spray the mozzarella over all the sticks and put for 2 to 3 min, under the grill till the cheese melts and make bubbles

Eat right away

Egg-free Coconut Flour Chaffles

Servings: 2
Cooking Time: 10 Minutes

Ingredients:

- 1 tablespoon flaxseed meal
- 2½ tablespoons water
- ¼ cup Mozzarella cheese, shredded
- 1 tablespoon cream cheese, softened
- 2 tablespoons coconut flour

Directions:

Preheat a waffle iron and then grease it.

In a bowl, place the flaxseed meal and water and mix well.

Set aside for about 5 minutes or until thickened.

In the bowl of flaxseed mixture, add the remaining ingredients and mix until well combined.

Place half of the mixture into preheated waffle iron and cook for about 3-minutes or until golden brown.

Repeat with the remaining mixture.

Serve warm.

Nutrition Info: Per Servings:
Calories: 76Net Carb: 2.3gFat: 4.2g Saturated Fat:
2.1gCarbohydrates: 6.3gDietary Fiber: 4g Sugar: 0.1gProtein: 3g

Buffalo Hummus Beef Chaffles

Servings: 4
Cooking Time: 32 Minutes

Ingredients:

- 2 eggs
- 1 cup + ¼ cup finely grated cheddar cheese, divided
- 2 chopped fresh scallions
- Salt and freshly ground black pepper to taste
- 2 chicken breasts, cooked and diced
- ¼ cup buffalo sauce
- 3 tbsp low-carb hummus
- 2 celery stalks, chopped
- ¼ cup crumbled blue cheese for topping

Directions:

Preheat the waffle iron.

In a medium bowl, mix the eggs, 1 cup of the cheddar cheese, scallions, salt, and black pepper,

Open the iron and add a quarter of the mixture. Close and cook until crispy, 7 minutes.

Transfer the chaffle to a plate and make 3 more chaffles in the same manner.

Preheat the oven to 400 F and line a baking sheet with parchment paper. Set aside.

Cut the chaffles into quarters and arrange on the baking sheet.

In a medium bowl, mix the chicken with the buffalo sauce, hummus, and celery.

Spoon the chicken mixture onto each quarter of chaffles and top with the remaining cheddar cheese.

Place the baking sheet in the oven and bake until the cheese melts, 4 minutes.

10. Remove from the oven and top with the blue cheese.
11. Serve afterward.

Nutrition Info:*Calories 552Fats 28.37gCarbs 6.97gNet Carbs 6.07gProtein 59.8g*

Cream Cheese Chaffle

Servings: 2
Cooking Time: 8 Minutes

Ingredients:

- 1 egg, beaten
- 1 oz. cream cheese
- ½ teaspoon vanilla
  4 teaspoons sweetener
- ¼ teaspoon baking powder
- Cream cheese

Directions:

Preheat your waffle maker.

Add all the ingredients in a bowl.

Mix well.

Pour half of the batter into the waffle maker.

Seal the device.

Cook for 4 minutes.

Remove the chaffle from the waffle maker.

Make the second one using the same steps.

Spread remaining cream cheese on top before serving.

Nutrition Info:
Calories 169Total Fat 14.3g Saturated Fat 7.6g Cholesterol 195mg Sodium 147mg Potassium 222mgTotal Carbohydrate 4g Dietary Fiber 4g Protein 7.7g Total Sugars 0.7g

Basic Sweet Chaffles

Servings: 1
Preparation Time: 1 Minute
Nutritional Values: 230 Kcal Calories | 18 G Fat | 3 G Carbs | 23 G Proteins

Ingredients

- 2 ounces of cream cheese
- 1 egg
- 1 tbsp of coconut flour
- 2 tsp of cocoa
- 1.5 tbsp of sweetener
- 1 tsp of vanilla
- 1/2 tsp of baking soda
- 1 tsp of cinnamon (not necessary)
- Oil Spray (Coconut)
- 1 tsp of butter (it's optional)

Directions

For 20 seconds, put cream cheese in a microwave protected bowl then microwave it. (If cream cheese is already at room temperature, this step is not required)

Add the remaining chaffle components with cream cheese into the dish

Socket-in and sprinkle your waffle iron with coconut oil

Just put enough of your combined ingredients on the waffle machine

Cover your maker, then patiently wait, yeah, that's going to be tough

Remove the cooked chaffle and place it on a tray

Top it with a butter slice

Buffalo Chicken Chaffle

Servings: 2-3
Preparation time: 15 minutes
Nutritional Value: 675 kcal Calories | 52 g Fat | 8 g Carbs | 44 g Proteins

Ingredients

- ¼ cup of almond flour
- 1 tsp of baking powder
- 2 large eggs
- 1/2 cup of shredded chicken
- ¼ cup of mozzarella cheese, crushed
- ¼ cup of Frank's Red-Hot Sauce plus 1 tbsp (optional)
- for topping ¾ cup of shredded cheddar cheese, sharp
- ¼ cup of crushed feta cheese
- ¼ cup of diced celery

Directions

Mix and beat the baking powder into almond flour in a medium mixing bowl, then put aside

Preheat your waffle maker on mid/high heat, then brush with low-carb non-stick spray generously

Put the eggs in a mixing bowl and whisk till foamy
Initially, insert in hot sauce & mix till well integrated

Transfer flour batter to eggs and blend till all mixed

Lastly, put in crumbled cheeses then mix well till combined

Mix in shredded chicken

Transfer chaffle mixture to preheated maker then cook till the outside browns. Approximately four minutes

Take it out from the waffle maker as well as perform step 7 till all the batter has been used up

Plate chaffles & it's top with celery, hot sauce or feta and serve

Keto Blt Avocado Chaffle Sandwich

Servings: 2-3
Preparation time:
20-30 minutes
Nutritional values: 208 kcal calories | 19.4g Fat | 3.1g Carbs | 20.3g Proteins

Ingredients

- 3-4 bacon pieces
- 1 egg
- 1/2 cup mozzarella
- 1 tsp flour of almonds
- 1 tsp of all Bagel Seasoning (or preferably a sprinkle of salt, garlic, onion powder)
- 2 lettuce slices
- 1 sliced tomato
- 1 avocado slice
- 1 tbsp mayonnaise

Directions
For Bacon

Start with a cold saucepan. Put the bacon in the pan and turn on the heat to a minimum. At minimum temperature, bacon cooks better.

When the bacon warms up a little bit and loses more of its fat, it begins curling up gently. You can then use tongs to rotate the bacon and start cooking on the other side. Then proceed to turn consistently until all sides of the bacon are fried, around 10 minutes for thin or up to 15 minutes for thicker sliced bacon.

For Sandwich

Plugin, the Mini Waffle maker, to preheat

Crack the egg into a little bowl to create the chaffle and blend along with 1/2 cup mozzarella, almond flour and all bagel seasoning. This blend produces 2 chaffles

Pour 1/2 of the mix into the preheated chaffle maker and permit 3-4 minutes of cooking (depending on how crispy you like your chaffles)

When cooking your first chaffle, prepare the tomato and avocado by cutting one slice of each

Pick up the chaffle and repeat for 3-4 minutes, adding the other half of the blend into the chaffle machine. When done, unplug the Waffle Machine

In the chaffle, add your fried Bacon, then finish with lettuce, tomato, avocado and mayo

Put 2 toothpicks in the chaffle to tie them together and slice them in half. Your chaffle BLT avocado is ready to serve now

Keto Chaffle Pizza

Servings: *2-3*
Preparation time: *15-20 minutes*
Nutritional Values: *76 kcal Calories | 4.3 g Fat | 1.2 g Carbs | 5.5 g Proteins*

Ingredients

- 1 egg
- 1/2 cup of crushed mozzarella cheese
- Only a pinch of seasoning, (Italian)
- 1 tbsp of pizza sauce (sugar-free)
- Topping with more crushed cheese pepperoni

Directions

Preheating the waffle machine

In the mixing bowl, beat the egg as well as seasonings together

Combine it with the crushed cheese and mix

To the hot waffle maker, insert a tablespoon of shredded cheese and then let it prepare for around 30 seconds. That will help produce a crisper crust

Apply half the batter to the machine then cook till it is golden brown & mildly crispy for around 4 min

To prepare the second chaffle, put the waffle out and insert the leftover mixture into the maker

Topping with pizza sauce, pepperoni and crushed cheese. Microwave it for around 20 seconds on high, and yes.

Chicken Quesadilla Chaffle

Servings: 1
Preparation time: 3 minutes
Nutritional values: 135 kcal Calories | 10 g Fat | 1 g Carbs | 11 g Proteins

Ingredients

- 1/3 cup of cooked shredded chicken
- 1 egg
- 1/3 cup of cheddar jack cheese, shredded
- 1/4 tsp of taco seasoning, homemade

Directions

Preheat your waffle maker

Mix the taco seasoning and egg in a little bowl. When combined, add the cheddar cheese and the diced chicken

In the waffle maker, put 1/2 of the mixture then cook for four minutes. Let them cook for yet another two min if they're still a little uncooked. Then cook the leftover batter to create another chaffle

4. Dip in sour cream, salsa or savor alone

Basic Mozzarella Chaffles

Servings: 2

Cooking Time: 6 Minutes

Ingredients:

- 1 large organic egg, beaten
- ½ cup Mozzarella cheese, shredded finely

Directions:

Preheat a mini waffle iron and then grease it.

In a small bowl, place the egg and Mozzarella cheese and stir to combine.

Place half of the mixture into preheated waffle iron and cook for about 2-minutes or until golden brown.

Repeat with the remaining mixture.

Serve warm.

Nutrition Info: Per Servings:

Calories: 5Net Carb: 0.4g Fat: 3.7g Saturated Fat: 1.5g

Carbohydrates: 0.4g Dietary Fiber: 0g Sugar: 0.2g Protein: 5.2g

Pumpkin Keto Chaffle Cake

Servings: 2
Preparation time: 10 min
Nutritional Value: 399 kcal Calories | 33 g Fat | 4 g Carbs | 11 g Proteins

Ingredients
For cake:

- 2 large eggs
- ¼ cup of pumpkin puree
- 2 tbsp of substitute brown sugar
- 2 tsp of pumpkin pie spice
- 2 tsp of coconut flour
- 1/2 tsp of vanilla
- 1 A cup of mozzarella cheese, finely shredded

For frosting:

- 4 oz of cream cheese, at room temperature
- ¼ cup of butter, at room temperature
- ½ cup of sweetener, powdered
- 1 tsp of vanilla
- ¼ cup of crushed pecans

Directions

Plug-in, to preheat waffle machine. Sprinkle with non - stick cooking spray

In a small bowl, add the pumpkin puree, eggs, sweetener

and pumpkin pie spice, vanilla, coconut flour and stir well

to mix

Mix in cheese

In the heated waffle iron, spoon one-fourth of the batter and spread the mixture out to the sides of the iron

Shut the iron and boil for 3 min

Take out and put aside the waffle. Repeat for batter left over

Let the chaffles cool down before frosting

Beat butter and cream cheese together with an electronic mixer till soft and moist, to prepare the frosting. Stir till mixed well, the powder sweetener plus vanilla

Pour the frosting on the top of a chaffle and cover with another chaffle. Repeat layers and end with a frosting layer

Scatter with crushed pecans to beautify

Brie And Blackberry Chaffles

Servings: 4
Cooking Time: 36 Minutes

Ingredients:

- For the chaffles:
- 2 eggs, beaten
- 1 cup finely grated mozzarella cheese
- For the topping:
- 1 ½ cups blackberries
- 1 lemon, 1 tsp zest and 2 tbsp juice
- 1 tbsp erythritol
- 4 slices Brie cheese

Directions:

1. For the chaffles:
2. Preheat the waffle iron.
3. Meanwhile, in a medium bowl, mix the eggs and mozzarella cheese.
4. Open the iron, pour in a quarter of the mixture, cover, and cook until crispy, 7 minutes.
5. Remove the chaffle onto a plate and make 3 more with the remaining batter.
6. Plate and set aside.
7. For the topping:
8. In a medium pot, add the blackberries, lemon zest, lemon juice, and erythritol. Cook until the blackberries break and the sauce thickens, 5 minutes. Turn the heat off.
9. Arrange the chaffles on the baking sheet and place two Brie cheese slices on each. Top with blackberry mixture and transfer the baking sheet to the oven.
10. Bake until the cheese melts, 2 to 3 minutes.
11. Remove from the oven, allow cooling and serve afterward.

Nutrition Info:
Calories 576Fats 42.22gCarbs 7.07gNet Carbs 3.67gProtein 42.35g

Hot Ham & Cheese Chaffles

Serving: 2-3
Preparation time: 5 minutes
Nutritional Values: 435 kcal Calories | 32 g Fat | 4 g Carbs | 31 g Proteins

Ingredients

- 1 large egg
- 1/2 cup of crushed swiss cheese
- 1/4 cup of deli ham, chopped
- 1/4 tsp of garlic salt
- 1 tbsp of mayonnaise
- 2 tsp of Dijon mustard

Directions

Plug it in to preheat the waffle iron

Beat the egg into a bowl. And add and combine in ham, cheese and garlic salt

In the heated waffle iron, put half of the batter, cover it and cook for 3-4 min or till the waffle iron finishes steaming as well as the waffle is prepared completely

Transfer the waffle to a tray and continue with the batter leftover

Mix the mustard and mayo together to use as a sauce

Break the waffles into half or quarters then serve with sauce

Turkey Chaffle Burger

Servings: 2
Cooking Time: 10 Minutes

Ingredients:

- 2 cups ground turkey
- Salt and pepper to taste
- 1 tablespoon olive oil
- 4 garlic chaffles
- 1 cup Romaine lettuce, chopped
- 1 tomato, sliced
- Mayonnaise
- Ketchup

Directions:

Combine ground turkey, salt and pepper.

Form thick burger patties.

Add the olive oil to a pan over medium heat.

Cook the turkey burger until fully cooked on both sides.

Spread mayo on the chaffle.

Top with the turkey burger, lettuce and tomato.

Squirt ketchup on top before topping with another chaffle.

Nutrition Info:
Calories 555Total Fat 21.5g Saturated Fat 3.5g Cholesterol 117mg Sodium 654mg Total Carbohydrate 4.1g Dietary Fiber 2.5g Protein 31.7gTotal Sugars 1g

Double Choco Chaffle

Servings: 2
Cooking Time: 10 Minutes

Ingredients:

- 1 egg
- 2 teaspoons coconut flour
- 2 tablespoons sweetener
- 1 tablespoon cocoa powder
- ¼ teaspoon baking powder
- 1 oz. cream cheese
- ½ teaspoon vanilla
- 1 tablespoon sugar-free chocolate chips

Directions:

Put all the ingredients in a large bowl.

Mix well.

Pour half of the mixture into the waffle maker.

Seal the device.

Cook for 4 minutes.

Uncover and transfer to a plate to cool.

Repeat the procedure to make the second chaffle.

Nutrition Info:
Calories 171Total Fat 10.7g Saturated Fat 5.3g Cholesterol 97mg Sodium
106mg Potassium 179mgTotal Carbohydrate 3g Dietary Fiber 4. Protein
5.8g Total Sugars 0.4g

Keto Pumpkin Chaffles

Servings: 2-3
Preparation Time: 2 min
Nutrition Values: 250 kcal Calories | 15 g Fat | 5 g Carbs | 23 g Proteins

Ingredients

- 1/2 cup of mozzarella cheese, shredded
- 1 egg beaten
- 1 1/2 tbsp of pumpkin purée
- 1/2 tsp of swerve
- 1/2 tsp of vanilla extract
- 1/4 tsp of pumpkin pie spice
- 1/8 tsp of maple extract, pure
- Optional: whip cream & sugar-free maple syrup, roasted pecans cinnamon, for topping

Directions

Switch on the Waffle Maker and begin the batter preparation

Insert in all the materials, with the exception of the mozzarella cheese, to a bowl and stir. Add the cheese in it and mix it so well

Sprinkle the waffle plate with a non-stick spray. Shut the lid, then cook for 4-6 mins depends on how crunchy you like the chaffles

Represent with any or some mix of toppings like butter, roasted pecans, sugar-free maple syrup, ground cinnamon dusting and a spoonful of whipped cream

NOTE

- You can also exclude this from the recipe if you do not have a pure maple extract, so they'll taste amazing!

Conquer Monsieur Or (Madame) Keto Chaffle Sandwich

Servings: *1-2*
Preparation time: *15 min*
Nutritional values: *360 kcal Calories | 18.4 g Fat | 9.5 g Carbs | 7.6 g Proteins*

Ingredients

- 2 chaffles
- Gruyere cheese with thin slices (enough for 3 layers)
- 2 thinly sliced strips of ham (or one thicker slice)
- 1-2 tsp Dijon mustard (or to taste)
- 1 pack keto bechamel sauce

Directions

Make use of the chaffles with the crispy, savory chaffle instructions

The broiler would be preheated on maximum. Put one of the chaffles on a grill rack in a baking dish. Add a layer of gruyere sliced and add a layer of ham sliced. Pour Dijon mustard over the ham. Apply a second layer of grated gruyere over the ham and put the second chaffle over it. Place the bechamel sauce over the top of the sandwich then place another sliced gruyere layer

Place the sandwich underneath the broiler before the cheese is melted, bubbly and light brown. Wait closely to guarantee it's not blackening

Take away from the frying pan. Simply cover with a freshly baked, sunny side up fried egg, served with a touch of salt and pepper if creating it into a Croque madame. Top it with fresh parsley and enjoy

Guacamole Chaffle Bites

Servings: 2
Cooking Time: 14 Minutes

Ingredients:

- 1 large turnip, cooked and mashed
- 2 bacon slices, cooked and finely chopped
- ½ cup finely grated Monterey Jack cheese
- 1 egg, beaten
- 1 cup guacamole for topping

Directions:

Preheat the waffle iron.

Mix all the ingredients except for the guacamole in a medium bowl.

Open the iron and add half of the mixture. Close and cook for 4 minutes. Open the lid, flip the chaffle and cook further until golden brown and crispy, minutes.

Remove the chaffle onto a plate and make another in the same manner.

Cut each chaffle into wedges, top with the guacamole and serve afterward.

Nutrition Info Per Servings:
Calories 311Fats 22.52gCarbs 8.29gNet Carbs 5.79gProtein 13.g

Cheeseburger Chaffle

Servings: 2
Cooking Time: 15 Minutes

Ingredients:

- 1 lb. ground beef
- 1 onion, minced
- 1 tsp. parsley, chopped
- 1 egg, beaten
- Salt and pepper to taste
- 1 tablespoon olive oil
- 4 basic chaffles
- 2 lettuce leaves
- 2 cheese slices
- 1 tablespoon dill pickles
- Ketchup
- Mayonnaise

Directions:

In a large bowl, combine the ground beef, onion, parsley, egg, salt and pepper.

Mix well.

Form 2 thick patties.

Add olive oil to the pan.

Place the pan over medium heat.

Cook the patty for 3 to 5 minutes per side or until fully cooked.

Place the patty on top of each chaffle.

Top with lettuce, cheese and pickles.

Squirt ketchup and mayo over the patty and veggies.

10. Top with another chaffle.

Nutrition Info:

Calories 325Total Fat 16.3g Saturated Fat 6.5g Cholesterol 157mg Sodium 208mg Total Carbohydrate 3g Dietary Fiber 0.7g Total Sugars 1.4g Protein 39.6g Potassium 532mg

Basic chaffle recipes

Here are four ways to create a basic chaffle. Chaffles work excellent as low carb keto bread, and they make fantastic low carb waffles, of course.

Servings: *1*
Preparation time: *2 minutes*
Nutritional values: *202 kcal Calories | 13 g Fat | 3 g Carbs | 16 g Proteins*

Ingredients

- 1 large egg
- 1/2 cup mozzarella cheese, finely grated

Directions

Preheat the waffle iron

Whisk up the one egg and the grated cheese with a fork in a tiny bowl unless mixed

Spread half of the mixture evenly well into the waffle

Cook for three or four minutes, or until golden brown. To cool, move onto a plate. Repeat the same for the remaining batter

Variations

- Use 2 egg whites or a modest 1/4 cup of carton white eggs for an egg white chaffle. Divide as instructed and prepare.
- Add 1/8 tsp maple extract to the egg / cheese mixture for a maple chaffle waffle.
- Add 1 tbsp of finely ground almond flour to an almond waffle chaffle.
  Mix it well. Divide as instructed and prepare.
- This recipe is for the most friendly degustation chaffles (with the exception of maple waffles). You can alter varieties with different cheeses, extracts and add-ins.

Other notes

- Store in the refrigerator in an airtight jar for up to 3-4 days. Reheat toaster in a toaster oven.

  Freeze each of the chaffles individually in plastic wrap and place them in zip-top freezer bags. Store up to 3 months. Reheat-thaw in the refrigerator overnight, or softly thaw in the microwave at low power. Then toast in an oven or toaster to get the texture back.

Keto Parmesan Garlic Chaffles – 3 Manner

Servings: _2_
Preparation Time: _2 minutes_
_Nutritional Values__: 352 kcal Calories | 24 g Fat | 2 g Carbs | 34 g Proteins_

Ingredients

- 1/2 cup of mozzarella cheese, shredded
- 1 beaten egg
- 1/4 cup of Parmesan cheese, grated
- 1 tsp of Italian Seasoning
- 1/4 tsp of garlic powder

Directions

Switch on your mini Waffle Maker

Bring in all the products, with the exception of the mozzarella cheese, to a bowl and mix. Put in the cheese and blend till it's mixed well

Spray non-stick spray on your waffle plates then add half of the batter in the center. Shut the cover as well as cook for 3 to 5 min, depends entirely on how crisp you want in your chaffles

There are a few choices to serve. One is to represent with grated parmesan cheese, a drizzle of olive oil and chopped fresh parsley or basil

NOTES
Transformations

- **Italian chaffle sandwich**

Start preparing the base recipe, as described above. Add lettuce and tomato, cold cuts and whatever you want to.

- **Chaffle breadsticks**

As mentioned above, make the base recipe. Slice each chaffle in 4 sticks then serve with sides of Marinara Sauce (low carb).

- **Chaffle bruschetta**

Start preparing the base mixture, as described above. Add 3 to 4 chopped cherry tomatoes, sliced, 1/2 tsp of chopped fresh basil and olive oil spray and a sprinkle of salt. Put over the upper part of the chaffles and serve as cooked above.

Mayonnaise & Cream Cheese Chaffles

Servings: 4
Cooking Time: 20 Minutes

Ingredients:

- 4 organic eggs large
- 4 tablespoons mayonnaise
- 1 tablespoon almond flour
- 2 tablespoons cream cheese, cut into small cubes

Directions:

Preheat a waffle iron and then grease it.

In a bowl, place the eggs, mayonnaise and almond flour and with a hand mixer, mix until smooth.

Place about ¼ of the mixture into preheated waffle iron.

Place about ¼ of the cream cheese cubes on top of the mixture evenly and cook for about 5 minutes or until golden brown.

Repeat with the remaining mixture and cream cheese cubes.

Serve warm.

Nutrition Info: Per Servings:
Calories: 190Net Carb: 0.6gFat: 17g Saturated Fat: 4.2gCarbohydrates: 0.8gDietary Fiber: 0.2g Sugar: 0.5gProtein: 6.7g

Keto Chaffle Pulled Pork Sandwich With Creamy Coleslaw

Servings: 4
Preparation time: 25 min.
Nutritional Value: 1000 kcal Calories | 48g Fat | 70g Carbs | 88g Proteins

Ingredients

- 1 pork butt - bone-in
- 8 tbsp barbecue sauce - free of sugar
- 1 packet of coleslaw mix or chopped cabbage
- 1 cup mayo
- 2 tbsp - heavy cream
- 1 tsp - creole mustard (any mustard you want, etc.)
- 1 tbsp erythritol. If you want a sweeter coleslaw, apply more erythritol (or any keto sugar substitute)
- 1 tsp (Optional) pepper
- 1 tsp garlic powder
- 1 tsp black chili pepper
- 1 tsp salt

Directions

1. Begins with "scoring" the roast's fat side. The scoring helps the seasoning to enter the fat and add this to another flavor

2. Use cooking oils, butter, mustard, Worcestershire sauce or any other chosen "wet" ingredient to add a slight element of moisture to enable the seasonings or rub to stick better to the meat

3. Cover the whole piece of meat absolutely with your favorite rub and let it sit for around 15-20 minutes until burning your Pit Barrel

4. Place the fat side of the pork butt on the grill so that the meat is covered, and the fat becomes crisper if you cut the pork into pieces for taste and texture pieces.

Smoke exposed inside until it hits 165 degrees. Put it in a foil tray, cover it and position it again in the cooker once 205 degrees is achieved

5. Take out the pan and let it cool. To remove the fat from the liquids, dump any liquid from the pan into another dish. Then place the juices back in the pan and start cutting the pork roast into medium-sized chunks and scraping any big fat or tendon pieces

6. Spray the same rub you cooked with over the pulled bits to provide a few extra spices and spray it with the cooking sauces

7. Combine all coleslaw dressing components and check taste for further changes to the seasoning. Toss the coleslaw (or cabbage mix) with the sauce. Coleslaw may appear thicker to begin with but will change for 1 hour while resting in the fridge.

8. Heat waffle iron for waffles. Drop one slice of cheese onto the waffle iron or scatter grated mozzarella cheese to cover the waffle maker's rim. Place 1/2 of a deviled egg over the cheese, which might melt. Place segmented cheese slice or cover with grated cheese and cover waffle iron. If you like it to be crunchier, let it steam for 3 minutes (until sides crisp) or more. When it cools, it can become crunchier, so check first to see what consistency you want and then change the period accordingly

9. Place chaffle sandwich together or eat in a bowl if you like to skip the chaffles

10. Use this remaining pulled pork at lunch for the next two days

CPSIA information can be obtained
at www.ICGtesting.com
Printed in the USA
BVHW010729220321
603169BV00013B/1202